TEACHING
TO
STRENGTHS

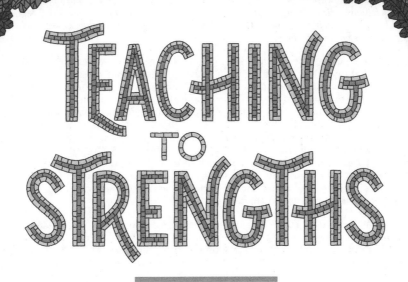

Teaching to Strengths

Supporting Students Living with Trauma, Violence, and Chronic Stress

Alexandria, Virginia USA

DEBBIE **ZACARIAN** | LOURDES **ALVAREZ-ORTIZ** | JUDIE **HAYNES**

1703 N. Beauregard St. • Alexandria, VA 223111714 USA
Phone: 800-933-2723 or 703-578-9600 • Fax: 703-575-5400
Website: www.ascd.org • E-mail: member@ascd.org
Author guidelines: www.ascd.org/write

Deborah S. Delisle, *Executive Director;* Robert D. Clouse, *Managing Director, Digital Content & Publications;* Stefani Roth, *Publisher;* Genny Ostertag, *Director, Content Acquisitions;* Carol Collins, *Senior Acquisitions Editor;* Julie Houtz, *Director, Book Editing & Production;* Liz Wegner, *Editor;* Donald Ely, *Senior Graphic Designer;* Mike Kalyan, *Director, Production Services;* BMWW, *Typesetter;* Kyle Steichen, *Senior Production Specialist*

PAPERBACK ISBN: 978-1-4166-2460-8   ASCD product #117035   n9/17
PDF E-BOOK ISBN: 978-1-4166-2462-2; see Books in Print for other formats.
Quantity discounts are available: e-mail programteam@ascd.org or call 800-933-2723, ext. 5773, or 703-575-5773. For desk copies, go to www.ascd.org/deskcopy.

Library of Congress Cataloging-in-Publication Data
Names: Zacarian, Debbie, author. | Alvarez-Ortiz, Lourdes, author. | Haynes, Judie, author.
Title: Teaching to strengths : supporting students living with trauma, violence, and chronic stress / authors: Debbie Zacarian, Lourdes Alvarez-Ortiz, and Judie Haynes.
Description: Alexandria, Virginia, USA : ASCD, [2017] | Includes bibliographical references and index.
Identifiers: LCCN 2017026472 (print) | LCCN 2017036527 (ebook) | ISBN 9781416624622 (PDF) | ISBN 9781416624608 (paperback)
Subjects: LCSH: Mentally ill children—Education. | Stress in children—Study and teaching.
Classification: LCC LC4165 (ebook) | LCC LC4165 .Z33 2017 (print) | DDC 371.94—dc23
LC record available at https://lccn.loc.gov/2017026472

26 25 24 23 22 21 20 19 18 17   1 2 3 4 5 6 7 8 9 10 11 12

In a very special way, we dedicate this book to the students and families we have had the honor to serve—particularly to those who inspired us to look for strengths hidden under adversity. We hope this book inspires you to do the same.

Teaching to Strengths

Introduction

Children and youth around the world are increasingly exposed to adverse childhood experiences that mark their lives profoundly. In the United States alone, half of the nation's total student population are students who have experienced or are experiencing trauma, violence, or chronic stress (National Survey of Children's Health, 2011/2012). This startling statistic should instantly raise the level of alarm about the epic number of preK–12 youth across every segment of the student population. The definitions below, drawn from family violence scholar Susan Craig (2008, 2016) and developmental and community psychologist Hirokazu Yoshikawa (2011), help us define what is meant by these three different terms and serve as a general description throughout our book.

Trauma: A response to an experience that is so stressful that it overwhelms an individual's capacity to cope.

Violence: The use of physical force to harm someone or to damage property; a great destructive force or energy.

Chronic stress: A physiological state of hyperarousal that can result in chronic anxiety, hypervigilance, and limits in regulating behaviors.

While much has been written about students experiencing these three phenomena, it is generally from a therapeutic perspective regarding how to provide adequate counseling supports and services for school-age learners who have experienced one or more of the following:

- Physical, sexual, or verbal abuse;
- Physical and emotional neglect;
- A parent who is an alcoholic (or addicted to other drugs);
- Witnessing a mother who experiences abuse;
- A family member in jail;
- Loss of a parent to death or abandonment, including abandonment by parental divorce; or
- Mental illness or a depressed or suicidal person in the home (Felitti et al., 1998; National Survey of Children's Health, 2011/2012).

While it is important for everyone to understand the various types of trauma, violence, and chronic stress and therapeutic supports for addressing them, very little professional literature has been written about *teaching* this segment of the population and doing so from a strengths-based perspective. In addition, the literature pays scant attention to diverse populations of students experiencing these circumstances in our rapidly evolving classrooms. Further, even less has been included about one of the fastest-growing segments in U.S. schools—English learners who experience these phenomena in distinct ways. Consider the following:

- In 2015, according to the U.S. Department of State, 69,933 refugees were admitted to the United States, with the largest groups coming from African, South Asian, Asian, and Latin American nations. Global crises (e.g., Syrians seeking refuge) show us all the shifting countries from which people flee and emphasize that we must be ready to face these changes.
- The U.S. Customs and Border Patrol (2015) reported that 107,000 undocumented minor children, ages 0–17, were apprehended crossing into the United States from Mexico—38,759 in fiscal year 2013 and

68,541 in 2014—a 77 percent increase in one year. A large proportion of these children are under 14 years of age.

- In 2016, the American Psychological Association reported that 4.1 million children born in the United States have at least one parent who is undocumented (Menjívar & Cervantes, 2016). Hirokazu Yoshikawa (2011), a renowned community and developmental psychologist and author of *Immigrants Raising Children,* found that many of the nation's children of undocumented immigrants experience high levels of chronic stress from fear of deportation, living in extreme poverty, and being isolated from peers.
- According to a 2013 Grantmakers for Education report, 60 percent of English learners' families had incomes that were 185 percent below poverty level.

This book is designed to be inclusive of the entire preK–12 population and, as such, pays special attention to students who come from diverse populations. By *inclusive,* we mean including those of us who work in urban, suburban, and rural settings with high and low incidences of students experiencing trauma, violence, and chronic stress. Further, it is our intention to support educators in adopting a teaching framework that is characterized by seeing, acknowledging, and capitalizing on the assets that students inherently bring versus what they do not. And in doing so, as educators, we are able to enhance the way that dynamically changing student populations perceive themselves, how they learn, and how we teach them.

Our book is distinctive in that it is written from a strengths-based perspective that draws from the personal, cultural, and world experiences that students and families bring with them and that can be capitalized on to create successful academic outcomes. Throughout the book, we use the terms *assets* and *strengths* interchangeably to denote the knowledge, skills, capacities, values, and attributes that all students possess. This is an important stance. Often, when we learn that students have experienced different types or degrees of trauma, violence, or chronic stress, we perceive them as having deficits that need remedying instead of focusing on the assets and capacities that are inherent to them or that they have already developed as a result of facing adversity. We also may perceive that families are too stressed or simply unable to help in our quest to support their children's learning and membership in their learning communities. When we take time to look more closely, differently, and empathetically, we find that many of these students and families have inherent strengths and remarkable degrees of social connectedness that support them during times of distress.

The purpose of this book is to provide an inclusive, comprehensive, collaborative approach for building teaching practices that support students' strengths, resiliency, and academic achievement—especially as it applies to the changing demographics that are occurring. Further, we want to examine how student learning can be enhanced when teachers, support staff, counselors, administrators, and other school community stakeholders work closely with students, families, and the community. Our special emphasis on teachers is a response to the reality that students spend the most significant amount of a school day with these professionals, and many teachers are looking for ways to be more effective in their work with this population.

The intended outcome of our book is to build teaching and schoolwide practices that, anchored in individuals' assets, support and enhance the academic and socio-emotional development of students living with trauma, violence, and chronic stress. Each chapter examines a critical element for doing this. Further, each shows how students' social and emotional learning can be supported and strengthened, and how overall learning can be enhanced, by (1) working with and caring for and about students living with these phenomena and (2) providing an asset-based instructional approach for students' socio-emotional and academic success.

Our book is intended for individuals and groups who work, or intend to work, in educational settings that serve preK–12 audiences (e.g., professional learning communities, book study groups, other in-service networks). In addition, we recommend this book for those involved in educator training, such as colleges and universities, educational service agencies, and district-based professional development efforts. The book's contents are also adaptable to classroom-level, building-level, and system-level foci in rural, suburban, and urban contexts. In addition, a special feature of the book is its real-world-from-the-field examples from educators living in various locations across the United States. Our purpose is to support the adaptation of these ideas to various professional environments.

Each chapter begins with an inspirational opening quote to reflect our strengths-based model. It then offers guiding questions to support the ideas, strategies, and principles we present. We also include a richly detailed snapshot of a student, family, or preK–12 classroom setting in a rural, suburban, or urban setting to situate ourselves in the real world of teaching. Another special feature of the book is the reflection activities included in the body of each chapter. These are intended to help readers apply and extend key ideas to their personal and professional lives. Our intent is that these reflection spaces be used for two types of audiences: (1) individual readers and (2) groups of readers, including participants in a college course, professional learning community, book group, or other collaborative activity.

The following are descriptions of the chapters in the book.

Chapter 1: The Urgent Need for a Strengths-Based Approach

We present the urgent need for using a strengths-based approach by drawing from students' inherent strengths and talents to support them in becoming confident, competent, and resilient learners. We examine key tenets of a strengths-based approach, incorporating research-based principles of positive psychology, positive youth development, neuroplasticity, and a growth mindset as they apply to students and families living with trauma, violence, and chronic stress. We also explore the essential need for instructional practices that support student learning and academic achievement through positive, asset-based relationships and interactions.

Chapter 2: Preparing to Work with Diverse Learners

We explore the preparatory steps needed to work with dynamically changing and diverse students and families living with trauma, violence, and chronic stress. In this chapter, we examine how educators can acknowledge their own unique experiences, take stock of their inherent strengths, and use these to learn and understand how their relationships and interactions with others affect this process. We also explore how educators can acknowledge the distinct experiences of this book's targeted population, identify and take stock of this population's inherent assets, and prepare to use a strengths-based instructional approach.

Chapter 3: Creating a Strengths-Based Classroom Learning Environment

This chapter looks more closely at the importance of teacher-student relationships, particularly as they apply to students living with trauma, violence, and chronic stress. We discuss key principles and strategies for creating a strengths-based classroom environment, including the following: teaching approaches that support student engagement and successful learning; connecting academic learning to students' personal, cultural, and world experiences; honoring what students bring to the classroom (rather than what they don't yet know); understanding the critical importance of routines, practices, and predictability to foster students' strengths and develop self-confidence; and developing the practice of a strengths-based gradual release of responsibility to bolster students' self-confidence as members of their classroom communities and as learners.

Chapter 4: Scaffolding Student-to-Student Relationships

In this chapter, we study the importance of asset-based student-to-student relationships, particularly as they apply to students who are living with trauma, violence, and chronic stress, as well as students who are not living with these phenomena. We look at key principles and strategies for creating, implementing, and reflecting on paired and small-group learning experiences. We also describe the importance of apprenticing students in the social and emotional communicative skills that are needed in collaborative learning settings. In addition, we explore the importance of using predictable routines and rituals in paired and small-group settings.

Chapter 5: Fostering Family/Guardian Engagement

We look closely at understanding and identifying families' strengths (from an unconscious competence to a conscious competence in using their strengths). We also provide practices and strategies for working more successfully and effectively with diverse students and families experiencing trauma, violence, and chronic stress.

Chapter 6: Infusing a Strengths-Based Approach Across a School

This chapter explores the importance of building an asset-based, collaborative, school-based team approach that includes students, families, teachers, support and administrative staff, and other school-based stakeholders. We also discuss the adoption of a strengths-based school approach and vision.

Chapter 7: Capitalizing on Community Assets to Build Partnerships

We examine building school/district and local community partnerships. We explore effective and continuous networking and collaborative partnerships with local community-based agencies and others serving students and families living with trauma, violence, and chronic stress, using our strengths-based approach.

The Urgent Need for a Strengths-Based Approach

It is an absolute human certainty that no one can know his own beauty or perceive a sense of his own worth until it has been reflected back to him in the mirror of another loving, caring human being.

—John Joseph Powell

Think back to when you formally trained to become an educator. How much time and how many course texts, readings, and activities were devoted to formally studying the complexities of working with students living with trauma, violence, and chronic stress? We often ask teachers this question when we provide professional development on the topic. Almost universally, across the United States, the common response we receive is that very little time or resources were devoted to studying this critical topic—especially as it applies to teaching students and working with their families. Rather, teachers tell us that they learn about what to do in four general ways: (1) by doing their best to teach students using trial-and-error strategies, (2) by learning from support staff, such as school counselors and others who engage in the psychosocial well-being of students, (3) by listening carefully at a school's child study team meetings when a variety of interpretations about students' and families' circumstances are discussed, and/or (4) by seeking advice from colleagues who have taught children with similar situations.

What exacerbates this situation even further is the reality that most educators have little to no formal education working with students and families who represent cultural, linguistic, racial, and economic experiences that are distinct from their own (Bransford, Darling-Hammond, & LePage, 2005; Darling-Hammond & Rothman, 2015). Whether it is working with high or low incidences of people who represent the rapidly growing diversity among U.S. students and their families, most educators tell us what the professional literature has confirmed for years: Very few in our profession have had any formal training or depth of experience working with the large, growing, and changing population of diverse learners—let alone those living with trauma, violence, and chronic stress.

The absence of any formal training in this area, understandably, has led many teachers to feel quite unprepared to teach and work with this population. Further, many teachers believe that some students' experiences are so extreme that there is little hope for them, despite all of the educators' efforts and good intentions. This perception often puts limits and restrictions on teachers in terms of how they teach and interact with students, as well as how they work with families. In a real sense, it has almost forced many teachers to look at students and their families as "broken" instead of as individuals who already possess inherent strengths and who can make great contributions to their classrooms, their communities, and the world. Indeed, for too long, teachers have found themselves using language to name their perceptions in terms of what they believe are impossible situations for students living with trauma, violence, and chronic stress. Here is an example.

While we were writing this chapter, one of us conducted a schoolwide training in an impoverished industrial city in the Northeast. She asked pairs of teachers to describe strategies that they found to be the most successful in their work with students living with trauma, violence, and chronic stress. While there were many different responses from each pair, one in particular resonated with the group. It went something like this: "I know that I am working hard, but it is impossible when I know that I have students who don't know whether they have a bed to sleep on at night, who worry about one of their parents who is incarcerated, or who come to school hungry." As you read this, you might find that you feel or have felt like this teacher. We acknowledge this reality, as well as the fact that many caring educators spend great amounts of their time and energy trying to minimize the effects of adversity on their students while simultaneously supporting them to succeed in school. Having said this, we also want to share our excitement about more recent evidence-based research that shows promising practices for teaching students living with trauma, violence, and chronic stress and working with their families. The foundation of this book is based on these findings.

What we propose is to take it a step further and look beyond "what is lacking" to find "what is already there" to effect change and sustain progress. Renowned pediatrician, professor of pediatrics at Children's Hospital of Philadelphia, and director of youth services at Covenant House Pennsylvania, Kenneth Ginsberg (2015) tells us that our students are "not broken" despite the many odds that they face. He urges us to look at our students in a different way so that we can see their many strengths and assets and tap into their natural resilience to improve their outcomes in school and beyond. An example that Ginsberg uses to illustrate this important point is his work with children who are chronically ill and their families. While he acknowledges the effect that chronic illness has on children's lives, he also points to the many strengths that the same children possess. Pushing his thoughts further, he discusses the importance of using these strengths to support students to become more confident, more competent, more connected and contributory to others, more committed to integrity, more able to cope, and able to have more control over their lives to make healthy choices.

In this spirit, we created the following question to embark on this transformational journey of teaching students living with trauma, violence, and chronic stress:

How can we move from feeling defeated, helpless, and hopeless in our beliefs about students experiencing trauma, violence, and chronic stress to being lighthouses of hope, high expectations, and appreciation of our students' and their families' inherent strengths?

Weaving Three Elements to Form a Braid of Understanding

In this chapter, we explore three critical and foundational elements for working effectively with students living with trauma, violence, and chronic stress. We use the illustration of three strands to show how interweaving these elements together forms a tight braid or bond. We have separated this chapter into the following three sections to reflect our braid framework.

1. The first section includes key evidence-based tenets of strengths-based teaching that we use to identify and acknowledge the inherent assets and capacities of students and their families to help us in creating and/or strengthening our teaching practices.

2. The second section is devoted to exploring some key principles for working with dynamically changing student and family populations. We examine some of the key concepts for understanding culture as a way of being and acting as it relates to child development.

3. The third section focuses on the importance of supporting student learning and thinking through interactions. We do so by drawing from the seminal contributions of developmental psychologist Lev Vygotsky (1978), who posited that student learning occurs through two interdependent systems: cognition and social interaction.

The intent of this chapter is to explore the possibilities that can occur when we use this braided framework. We draw from it to build on students' inherent strengths, connect with their cultural ways of being, and create opportunities for students to learn through interactions to expand their ability to cope and help them become confident learners and active members of their classrooms, school communities, and beyond.

Let's begin by engaging in a reflection activity intended to help us explore some key principles about students living with trauma, violence, and chronic stress. As we stated in the Introduction, all of the reflection activities found in the book are intended for applying and extending the key ideas to our personal and professional lives. They are also intended for two types of audiences: individual readers and groups of readers, such as those in a college course, professional learning community, or book study group.

 Time for Reflection

Read the following descriptions of three different 9th grade classmates attending an urban high school in a southwestern U.S. state and respond to the subsequent reflection questions.

David was born in the United States. Many years ago, his older brother and parents crossed the Mexican border without documents. For this reason, they live in constant fear of being deported. David and his family have moved many times. In school, David generally earns *B* grades with an occasional *C*, and his teachers describe him as a pleasant and hardworking student.

Brianna is the oldest of three siblings and lives with her grandmother. When Brianna was in 7th grade, her mother was killed in a car accident. We have been asked to observe Brianna in class and see that she tries to follow her teacher's directions diligently. We also observe Brianna's mathematics teacher correcting her on a problem set that she has just completed. Pointing to the board at the correct formula for solving the problem, her teacher says to Brianna, "You will want to use this formula for substitution on the Pythagorean theorem." Upon hearing this, Brianna breaks down in tears. We also note her classmates moving away from Brianna and a few stating, "There she goes again."

Jasmine is an only child who lives with her parents. Jasmine's father has been in and out of drug treatment facilities for alcohol and drug addiction and the prison system for related offenses. Most recently, he was released from the local jail after a fistfight that he instigated at a local bar. We learn that Jasmine has witnessed several acts of violence between her parents—particularly her father against her mother. Her teacher reports to us that Jasmine rarely misses school and that when she works in groups with other students, she often seems to pick an unprovoked fight with her classmates.

1. What assets can you identify in each student?

2. How might you draw from these assets in your work with students?

Using a Strengths-Based Instructional and Interactional Approach

Research points to the urgent need to approach the topic of students living with trauma, violence, and chronic stress from a more positive stance, as opposed to looking at it through a deficit-based lens. The field of psychotherapy suggests that focusing on people's inherent strengths (what they bring) has been proven to lead to better outcomes than focusing on what we perceive as their weaknesses (Seligman, Rashid, & Parks, 2006). In educational settings, additional research shows that we can help students be more successful and engaged when we draw from their internal strengths and capacities (Biswas-Dienera, Kashdan, & Gurpal, 2011). Part of our thinking needs to shift from what we believe is not happening and impossible to what is happening and possible. To do this we must take time to

- Identify students' existing strengths.
- Honor, value, and acknowledge these strengths.
- Help students become aware of their strengths.
- Build instructional programming that boosts social ties and networks by drawing from students' strengths.

These four elements are essential to teaching students living with trauma, violence, and chronic stress. And they bring us back around to the first reflection task.

How easy was it to identify the various strengths of the students? Many educators tell us that it is challenging for them to find any strengths for the last student, Jasmine. They have shared with us that they just don't see how her circumstances and what she does in school reflect any assets. So let's go back to Jasmine for a few moments before we enter into a discussion about the principles of positive psychology. In the description, we share that Jasmine comes to school every day. If we think about this, despite whatever we perceive about her home life (and we have not furnished much about it in terms of the relationships that she has with her mother, neighbors, family's community, and more), she is coming to school regularly, consistently, and routinely. This is certainly a strength that she possesses. It shows responsibility, value for education, value for interactions, hope, appreciation, gratitude, determination, connection, and courage, to name a few of her values and qualities. What this points us toward is the research encouraging us to look for specific student strengths so that we may draw from these in our work.

Psychologist Abraham Maslow's (1999) contributions help us understand the possibilities of what can occur when we look through our strengths-based lens.

Principles of positive psychology. Maslow (1999) pioneered the idea of looking at human behavior through the lens of the assets, capacities, and qualities that empower people and their communities to flourish. He coined the term *positive psychology* to reflect this idea. Positive psychology is a belief that, as humans, we all want to be the best that we can be and that it is in our nature to strive toward what Maslow refers to as our *self-actualized* potential. It positions human behavior as being driven by the desire to lead richly meaningful and fulfilling lives. Further, it does not ignore or dismiss the need to take time to understand the difference between what helps us achieve our potential and what doesn't. While not abandoning their roles as scientists of healing, experts in positive psychology (also referred to as positivists) argue that we have to give as much attention to acknowledging and building positive qualities as we have given to repairing damage (Morris & Maisto, 2002). In addition, positive psychology expands beyond the self. It looks closely at the human potential for working and collaborating together. Interpersonal relationships, according to Maslow, are made more possible when we believe in each other's worth or value and when we mutually support each other to see our collective human potential.

Earlier, we acknowledged that many caring educators spend great amounts of their time and energy trying to minimize the effects of adversity on their students while simultaneously supporting them to succeed in school. Part of this is our capacity to be empathetic educators; that is, educators who understand our students' circumstances and seek ways to make education meaningful for those students. The tenets of positive psychology require that we be empathetic *and* asset-based teachers. First, we must have an understanding of our students, and second, we must work from their strengths.

Here is a small example that will be expanded on later in the book. Let's say that we are David, Brianna, and Jasmine's U.S. history teacher. In our course text, students are reading about the U.S. Civil War. The text talks about fathers and sons leaving their families to fight in the war. One of the activities created by the school district's history department asks students to interview their parents about what it would be like to leave a family member behind to fight in a war. As empathetic teachers, we likely would know that some students don't live with their parents. Indeed, Brianna lives with her grandmother. With this knowledge, we would modify the question to be more inclusive of all of our students, including Brianna and others. The same would hold true for making modifications for students who are homeless or living in shelters, or whose parent or guardian is deployed to an area of conflict, so that what we do is inclusive, respectful, validating, and honoring. In addition, if we changed the earlier examples to include a student who is an unaccompanied minor from a war-torn country and learning English, we would make second language learning modifications (such as asking a question that matches the student's level of English proficiency or asking it in the student's native language). We would also modify the question to be relevant and sensitive to the student's background. Furthermore, we would anchor all of these modifications on the students' previously identified assets. While later chapters explore these ideas in much more detail, the point here is that the foundational principles of positive psychology mean working from an empathetic understanding of students *and* their strengths. Further, we are drawing from these to bolster our students' confidence and motivation as learners.

Principles of positive youth development. One of the most exciting aspects of being an educator is supporting all students to draw from their strengths and capacities to develop the skills, competencies, and confidence to be active learners, independent and critical thinkers, and invaluable members of their learning community, local community, and beyond. It calls for creating a classroom and school environment where everyone is seen as already capable, already learning, and already contributing (Zacarian & Silverstone, 2015). Positive youth development (PYD) supports this way of thinking. Foundational to PYD is a belief that children's outcomes are not inevitable or predictable based on what we perceive their circumstances to be. Core to PYD are two foundational principles:

1. All students and families bring great assets and capacities.

2. The human brain has a great capacity to build new pathways for being and acting (Floyd & McKenna, 2003; Lerner, Almerigi, Theokas, & Lerner, 2005).

Let's look at the first element—that all students and families bring great value to learning. Moll, Amanti, Neff, & Gonzalez (1992) coined the term *funds of knowledge* to describe the expertise that families bring to their children's learning. They conducted research on families living in the border region between the United States and Mexico. Where some might say that the families were uneducated and therefore could not help their children in school, the researchers found the opposite. The families they studied possessed very high levels of knowledge and skills that related to their work, home life, and well-being. Further, and more importantly, these families passed the knowledge and skills on to their children. What is critical for us to consider as we begin to explore students living with trauma, violence, and chronic stress is that their school lives can be productive, positive, and fulfilling when we see the assets and strengths that students and families bring.

A second and equally critical component to working with students and families experiencing these phenomena is that, as humans, we have the capacity to overcome the odds stacked against us. The scientific notion of neuroplasticity points to the brain's capacity to create new pathways. The latest advances in the field of neuroscience suggest the ability of the brain to "rewire itself," under certain conditions, giving us an enormous amount of hope in our work with students who have experienced trauma. What is important for educators to consider is how we contribute to creating an environment that capitalizes on this newly discovered inherent strength to benefit students and families.

Using a growth mindset with students living with trauma, violence, and chronic stress. World-renowned Stanford psychologist and researcher Carol Dweck (2006) created the idea of a *growth mindset*. She defines it as believing that students can succeed when we teach them in four specific ways:

1. When we specifically teach students to believe in their abilities to embrace the challenges and complexities of learning.

2. When we show students the value and purpose of being persistent.

3. When we show students that we value effort as a positive.

4. When we inspire students to do more.

Each requires us to be positive in the language that we use, positive in our intent, and positive in our belief that all students can succeed. In a real sense, it means that we, too, have to possess the same four ways of thinking on behalf of student learning.

Dweck contrasts having a *growth mindset* with having a *fixed mindset,* whereby we believe that there are always some students who cannot succeed—such as the teacher who felt hopeless about his students and helpless in teaching them that we referenced at the beginning of the chapter. The point is, once we have these fixed mindsets, it is almost a self-fulfilling prophecy that we cannot change and therefore cannot help our students succeed because we are convinced that nothing we do will work. According to sociologist Claude Steele (2010), these perceptions can and do negatively go so far as to affect some students who perceive themselves to be in a racial, ethnic, linguistic, cultural, economic, or gender group that is not expected to show school success. Just think of this fixed mindset as it applies to what we believe about students and what students believe about themselves or their peers.

As educators, our individual perspectives always benefit from another point of view. None of us has all of the answers—especially regarding the complexities of teaching students and working with families experiencing trauma, violence, and chronic stress. We tend to see a partial picture of any whole. As such, it requires the support of others to help us see what is really there. Take, for example, Brianna, the second student we described, who cried during her mathematics class when her teacher asked her for information about how she had solved a problem set. As educators, we have a pivotal role in fostering an open and much-needed dialogue with students, families, colleagues, supervisors, and other stakeholders to ensure that what we do works for our students. While we know Brianna is hardworking, think of how much might be gained by engaging in a growth mindset dialogue with Brianna to help support her to embrace the challenges of learning math; acknowledge, honor, and value her persistence and desire to do well; show her how her efforts are valued; and learn how we might inspire her to do more.

Our first step is believing in students' inner strengths; our second is identifying these strengths. Knowing that we are working with students from a wide array of personal, cultural, language, and economic experiences, we must be open to understanding and appreciating the various cultures of others. When we allow ourselves to be influenced and changed by different perspectives, and when we see these as strengths rather than obstacles, we embrace a growth mindset and, in turn, begin working toward a transformation model on behalf of our students. This leads us to the second of our three interwoven strands: the importance of understanding culture as a way of being and acting.

Understanding Culture as a Way of Being

Developmental psychologist Mary Gauvain (2001) helps us understand the critical importance of a family's cultural community in terms of children's development. Knowing that we are working with diverse and dynamically changing student and family populations, including students living with trauma, violence, and chronic stress, it is important to understand the various cultural communities represented in our local contexts. Here are some important features to consider when thinking about the importance of a family's cultural community.

Children are guided to participate in their family's community and beyond both actively (e.g., engaging in family discussions) and passively (e.g., observing their family at home and in groups such as at a church ritual). Children learn how to act and behave through repeated exposure to, observation of, and interactions with their home and family communities. In contemporary society, the term *parents/guardians*, for example, has many meanings, including children being raised by two parents, a single parent, a blended family, grandparents, unrelated people who live cooperatively, or foster parents, and children being raised with significant support from extrafamilial individuals

(Zacarian & Silverstone, 2015). The same holds true for the many different groups with which children routinely interact. In this sense, culture refers to the places where students interact to gain meaning from the world around them. As such, child development involves interactions between and among children, their parents/guardians, family, family's community, school community, local community in which they are reared, and beyond. Figure 1.1 illustrates the type of interactions that occur during a typical child's development.

A growing number of school-age children are being reared in situations where violence, trauma, and chronic stress have had or are having a significant adverse effect on their development. This is not to say that all school-age children who experience trauma, violence, and chronic stress have these outcomes; the effect of these phenomena varies greatly. Factors such as students'

Figure 1.1 | Circles of Interactions

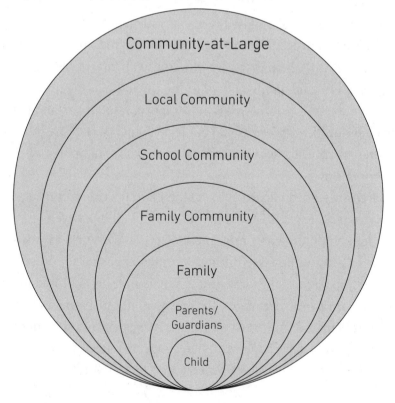

age and level of development; culture; prior exposure to and experience with trauma, violence, and stress; and any pre-existing conditions that might affect a student or a student's family are all relevant (Cole et al., 2005; Presidential Task Force on Posttraumatic Stress Disorder and Trauma in Children and Adolescents, 2008). In addition, and of critical importance, are (1) the inherent strengths that many students already possess and (2) the external supports that they receive from others of unconditional trust and care (Ginsberg & Jablow, 2015). What is it that greatly helps these two critical elements occur? Interactions—consistent, routine, predictable, nurturing, and stimulating interactions, and lots of them. As shown in Figure 1.1, these include an ever-growing, ever-widening developmental circle of interactions.

Indeed, students are exposed to many social connections/networks and interactions in their everyday lives. These occur over and over again and serve as the cement or glue that binds their development. Thus far in this book, we have pointed to the critical importance of students' inherent strengths and interactive capacities. Let's look back at the first student we described at the beginning of this chapter, David Martinez, to further illustrate what we mean about culture as a way of being and acting.

David was born in the United States, and the undocumented status of his older brother and parents causes the whole family to live in constant fear of being deported. As empathetic educators, we understand the anxiety and chronic stress that the family is experiencing and want to support David to feel and be welcomed unconditionally in our classroom. With this said, let's add a few more details about David and his family in our quest to see their many strengths. He and his family have moved multiple times for several important reasons. First, they live in extreme poverty. At times, they live in cramped places with unrelated people in their attempt to secure shelter. They have lived in cars. They have spent small amounts of time living in apartments on their own. They are always on the move because of their concerns about being caught by the authorities, and they have never sought the types of nutritional, medical, legal, or housing support that many low-income U.S. citizens receive. Also, David's parents and brother do not possess social security cards or any legal documents out of fear that these would require them to declare their undocumented immigration status. As such, while we might believe that David is being reared without many of the social ties and interactions that many of us have probably experienced, he has had and is having a number of meaningful, continuous interactions with the various networks of people that are in his life. Here is an example.

Every week, David and his family go to the laundromat that is closest in proximity to where they are living. They look forward to this ritualized activity. If we were to ask David what his favorite place is, he would tell us the laundromat. So let's say that we go with him every week and observe him and his family engaging in the weekly activity. What would we see? We would see him and his family having lively conversations with other children and adults while they all wait for the cleaning activity to be completed. These interactions and relationships reflect the collectivist culture in which David is being reared.

What do we mean by collectivist? Research on educational practices show a distinction between a mainstream cultural belief that favors individualism and competition and a minority belief that favors collectivism and relation-ships as a way of being and acting (Tyler et al., 2008). If we look at David through this lens, he is being reared in a culture that favors collectivism and relationships. His family goes to the local laundromat for more than doing their laundry. They go as members of a collectivist culture to cultivate this culture. Indeed, they also gain invaluable support from these gatherings, as many of the families they meet experience similar joys and adversities.

Generally, but not always, a family's community represents its cultural, linguistic, racial, and economic experiences. The interactions they engage in as members of the community further cement children's understanding of the world around them, as do the rules and mores of the culture in which they are being reared (Rogoff, 2003). In this sense, David's understanding of the world around him comes from these rituals of interactions that his family engages in on a regular basis with the communities at the laundromat.

Let's push this a little further. David speaks two languages fluently, Spanish and English, and he often acts as his parents' interpreter. For example, when they move, David regularly engages in conversations with the family's landlord, as many do not speak Spanish. Because they move on a regular basis, he is deeply familiar with the rituals associated with moving in and out of various domiciles. In fact, if we observe David regularly, we see that he is quite adept at negotiating the rent and other activities that help his family's living circumstances. In a great sense, David's personal, world, cultural, and literacy knowledge is being nurtured by the practices that he experiences at home, at the laundromat, and elsewhere.

Following this train of thought, ideally when he goes to school, he engages in interactions that show him that his background experiences are valued by his school community, which includes his teachers, peers, administrators, school counselors, specialists, and so forth. And as David grows up, his world grows larger to include his local city's community and beyond. Through adolescence, even though he may spend significantly less time with his parents and his family's communities, it is these circles of influence that represent what we know as students' cultural ways of being and acting (Zacarian, 2013).

Let's look at the assets that David brings.

The positive effect of social ties and interactions. David comes from a loving family that wants him to receive a good education and do well in school. As representatives of a collectivist culture, they believe in the importance of providing David and themselves with rich opportunities to engage with others. At the laundromat, David's family provides him with a high level of interactive social and networking supports. We use the word *networking,* as he is continuously and critically engaging in interactions. Indeed, each of these interactive experiences that he engages in provides him with the opportunity to extend his understanding of the world around him. In a sense, as educators, we have to think of this in terms of the interactive spheres of influence that support our students to learn.

Figure 1.2 shows the various spheres of interactive influence and social networking that David engages in. Each person provides him, in his or her unique ways, with multiple opportunities to engage in interactions and to understand the world he lives in and how to thrive as well as flourish in it.

Figure 1.2 | Spheres of Interactive Influence and Social Networking

Parents

Local
Community

Family

David

School
Community

Family
Community

Classroom
Community

 Time for Reflection

1. What teaching strategies might you use based on these spheres of interactive relationships in which David engages?

2. In what ways would these support David to learn?

3. How would these strategies capitalize on David's assets?

Supporting Thinking Through Social Interactions

Our third strand refers to the essential role of supporting thinking through social interactions. Social interaction was one of the key elements for Lev Vygotsky's (1978) social development theory. Vygotsky, a developmental psychologist renowned for his contributions about learning, stated that two systems must be operationalized for learning to occur:

1. Cognition
2. Social interaction

The first system, cognition, is built from prior knowledge or understanding. In school settings, we might refer to this as the subject matter being studied or method of learning being used, in combination with our students' personal, cultural, communicative, and world knowledge experiences. The second system, social interaction, we learn by communicating with others. It is equally important as the first. It requires students to interact with teachers, each other, family, their community, and beyond to have the rich opportunity to use language to learn. Figure 1.3 illustrates these two systems in formula form: cognition plus social interaction equals learning. A good example is David's demonstrated capacity to be a strong member in collaborative group settings. Through his understanding of and interactions participating in a collectivist culture, he has shown the capacity to work well with others by being patient, attentive, an active listener and speaker, a good negotiator, and more.

As such, learning is both an internal (cognitive) and external (communicating with others) process. It requires us to support students living with trauma, violence, and chronic stress and bolster their instructional programming in multiple ways. First, to get students thinking, we have to know about their personal, cultural, language, and world experiences. That is, we must support students in building connections with the content that is being taught with what they already know. In doing so, we capitalize on students' assets and guide and encourage them to navigate more challenging territory with our support. This relates to Vygotsky's (1978) *zone of proximal development.* As educators, we need to continuously look for ways to provide students with multiple strengths-based opportunities to interact. In other words, if we know that learning involves social interactions, what can we do to ensure that these occur routinely and regularly?

The key to making learning work is using the foundation of our braid framework. That is, adopting a strengths-based approach whereby teachers identify and acknowledge the assets and capacities of students, understand and value their cultural ways of being, and support and create opportunities for learning through thinking and social interactions.

The next chapter explores the preparatory steps needed to work with dynamically changing diverse students and families living with trauma, violence, and chronic stress by focusing more closely on our first strand.

Figure 1.3 | Formula for Learning

Preparing to Work with Diverse Learners

The secret of change is to focus all of your energy not on fighting the old but on building the new.

—Socrates

We all face adversity of one type or other throughout our lives. It can come at us like a whimper or hit us unexpectedly like a freight train. One of the unique aspects of applying a strengths-based approach to our personal lives and, particularly, our professional lives as educators is that each of these *adversity encounters* has the potential to bring our strengths to the surface while helping us cope and become more resilient. Equally important is our capacity to help students in developing and applying a strengths-based approach that acknowledges and values their internal strengths (i.e., what they already possess) while helping them cope and become more resilient.

This chapter explores the preparatory steps to take in working with students and families living with trauma, violence, and chronic stress when using an asset-based approach. We acknowledge the effects that these phenomena can and do have on students and families and the secondary stress that results for many educators. In this chapter, we take it a step further and look at these students as having abundant internal strengths that they can draw from and rely on. Teachers, too, must navigate through difficult situations. For many of us, it does not come naturally to look for the positive values and qualities in people. Many of us find ourselves spending a great deal of time and effort looking at what isn't happening, as opposed to the positives of what is occurring.

According to Pulla (2012), many professions, including education, are too focused on what is wrong. As educators, we were trained to look at, assess, and remedy the academic skills that students are weak at, what they do not know or do not have. There is nothing wrong with that. But we also need to assess the skills that the very same students have been able to develop so we can help build new skills on the existing foundation. Students living with trauma, violence, and chronic stress are understandably perceived as lacking the emotional well-being that their peers may exhibit. It is not this book's intention to undermine the adverse effect these experiences inflict on students. The research is very clear on this, but the research has also demonstrated that the brain is malleable and brain chemistry can be altered through positive and consistent connections with trusted adults. If we fixate on seeing the "damage," we might miss the assets, strengths, and positive qualities that exist behind it.

A strengths-based approach supports our efforts in looking for, finding, and securing ways to identify what is right, thus taking care of ourselves, our overall well-being, and our students (Pulla, 2012). Indeed, focusing much-needed energy and effort on a strengths-based approach calls for us to see this as an essential way to open wide the doors of possibilities rather than keep them only partially open or even shut. We have the moral responsibility to recognize our own biases, attitudes, and limitations in adopting a more positive, asset-based approach when interacting with other adults as well as with our students. Why? As we will see in this chapter, we are more effective agents of change when we cultivate our own and others' strengths and assets than when we ignore them or dismiss them as being of lesser importance.

This chapter shows how to prepare for using strategies and approaches to help work with our targeted population. First, we examine our own unique experiences, take stock of our assets and strengths, and use these to learn and understand how our relationships and interactions with others affect this process. We then explore ways in which we can examine the unique experiences of our targeted population, identify and take stock of this population's assets and strengths, and prepare to use a strengths-based instructional approach. We will see that understanding and drawing from our strengths greatly helps us in creating instructional techniques, strategies, and interventions that stem from this strengths-based approach. The chapter looks closely first at teachers and then at students.

Reframing Personal Perceptions from Deficit to Abundance

Defining our own values and assets in both positive and challenging situations is important to consider. To get started, complete the following reflection activity. The reflection activities found throughout the book are intended to apply and extend the key ideas to our personal and professional lives and for individual readers and groups of readers, such as those in a college course, professional learning community, or book study group.

 Time for Reflection

1. Identify and describe a positive experience you had in the last few years.

2. Describe the values that were represented in this amazing experience.

3. Identify the values and qualities you demonstrated during this experience. Use Figure 2.1 to help you identify them or add your own.

The idea behind this type of reflective thinking is that it affirms, for each of us, the internal strengths that we have or were able to identify through the support of others who stood close to us during these positive experiences. Let's say, for example, that one person wrote about his experience completing a college degree to become a professional educator. Let's add three qualities that he used to describe the experience: affirmation, perseverance, and self-sacrifice. These reflect the internal strengths that he possesses and that allowed him to stay the course, believe in himself, delay gratification, and beat frustration to achieve a goal. It highlights some of his personal qualities that were key in having such a positive experience.

Now engage in a second reflection activity, one that focuses on a difficult situation.

Figure 2.1 | Values and Qualities Worth Acknowledging

• Acceptance	• Faith	• Nonjudgment
• Adaptability	• Flexibility	• Passion
• Affirmation	• Friendship	• Perseverance
• Commitment	• Generosity	• Professionalism
• Courage	• Honesty	• Relaxation
• Daring	• Honor	• Resilience
• Depth	• Humility	• Respect
• Differentiation	• Humor	• Sacrifice
• Discretion	• Industriousness	• Self-control
• Endurance	• Insight	• Validation
• Energy	• Loyalty	• Value
• Experimentation	• Mindfulness	• Wit

Source: Adapted from Glasser (2011, pp. 64–65).

Time for Reflection

1. Identify and describe a difficult moment you experienced in the last few years.

2. Provide some details about what brought you into this negative moment.

3. Explore all the negative things you could have done that you chose not to do.

4. Why did you stop yourself from engaging in that layer of negative behaviors?

When we experience a challenge and are upset at the prospect of it or of addressing it, we are often driven by underlying values and qualities, even though they do not seem evident at first. Furthermore, we possess values and attributes that often stop us from making bigger mistakes or poor choices. Let's look at an example of a teacher, Laura Reynolds. Let's say that Laura identified a difficult moment in her life working with students living with trauma, violence, and chronic stress. She wrote about how difficult it was for her to be accountable for students who miss so many days of school. This led to her expressing exasperation with being a teacher and wanting to leave the profession. However, what initially seems to be a negative experience loaded with emotions proves to be a showcase of her values and attributes.

Let's look closer at Laura. She felt very upset because she was worried about her students' lives inside and outside of the school environment (caring). She worried about their future and their learning (commitment, sensitivity, responsibility, passion, sacrifice) and felt she needed to be there for them. Among the things she could have done negatively, but chose not to do, was leave the profession and find a less stressful job. Why did she stop herself from making those choices? Values and attributes such as her commitment to underprivileged students, her unselfishness and dedication, and her strong religious values that encourage her to help others in need underlie her reactions in this difficult moment. All these positive attributes (and we could keep highlighting more) were hidden, but still present, in this difficult moment.

Applying an Open-Door Framework

Using a strengths-based model allows us to see real possibilities. It does not mean that we are not cognizant of obstacles; indeed, these are important to acknowledge. We are not dismissing or discounting them or the anguish that they cause. Social work scholar Dennis Saleebey (2000) points to this as a binary stance: acknowledging real challenges that we and our students experience but centering our energy on extracting and finding the underlying goodness that each individual brings with them. We must be intentional in our attempts to energize or reward only positive choices, decisions, and behaviors. We must also be careful not to accidentally energize or reward negativity. A simple example of energizing negativity is an educator who lectures a student for being late to school. Through this interaction the student learns that to earn his teacher's valuable attention and energy, he just needs to engage in negative behavior. As Grove and Glasser (2007) indicate, "We tend to demonstrate much more evidence of energy and relationship when things are going wrong instead of producing that energy and relationship in response to successes" (p. 18). In our example, the perfect opportunity for the teacher to genuinely invest energy and attention in acknowledging the responsibility displayed by the student is when the student gets to school on time. Indeed, it is when students display positive behaviors that we should be generous with our energy, acknowledgment, and interaction.

The image of an open door illustrates what is possible using a strengths-based approach. Chapter 1 described the means by which we all develop. We interact with others. Our personal, social, cultural, and world views are rooted in our interactive experiences with others. Indeed, we draw from these to develop our own unique perspectives, approaches, and concepts of who we are. In a great sense, who we are as individuals is shaped by these experiences. Our strengths, our assets, and our capacities to support our own well-being and that of others are based on our own uniqueness. In this spirit of an open door, as well as our unique individual qualities and characteristics, complete the following activity by looking reflectively at the terms you used in the two earlier reflection activities to describe your experiences. Look inward at the values underlying both situations, the positive and the negative, and how you used them to learn about your assets. While looking inward, examine the words you used to describe the situations.

Time for Reflection

1. Consider the descriptors that you used from Figure 2.1 or that you came up with on your own. How do these describe your inherent strengths and capacities to address these situations?

2. How did this reflection task help support you in affirming, discovering, or enhancing your strengths?

When . . . Then . . . Theory of Change

Foundational to using a strengths-based approach is believing in it throughout all that we do as educators. Think of it as a *When . . . Then . . .* proposition. What does this mean? *When* we believe that every human being is valuable and possesses many strengths, *then* we intentionally look for these strengths and support individuals in using these for their personal growth. This theory of change allows or frees us to focus on identifying, acknowledging, and "mobilizing and honoring the resources, assets and wisdom and knowledge that every person, family group or community has" (Pulla, 2012, p. 53). The alternative—that is, choosing to use a deficit-based model—will continue to be harmful to our own well-being and, more importantly, that of our students.

A first step in this process is taking time to acknowledge our own strengths in positive and challenging situations. The reflection activities provided earlier in the chapter were targeted for us to refocus our professional and personal energies in this direction. When we see positives, we create more positives. Again, we are not dismissing what is there or ignoring it. We're focusing our energies on finding the positives that are also there and using these to support our personal growth. We suggest the following:

1. Periodically, take time to re-engage in the three reflection activities from earlier in the chapter. Yes, go through the whole process again. It will greatly help in reaffirming your strengths.

2. Use your findings to reignite your identified strengths and capitalize on them. The process is not intended to be repetitive. Rather, it is intended to provide the much-needed energy to engage in your work as an educator.

3. Use a When . . . Then . . . approach. Here are some suggestions for using it on a regular basis:

When I identify my strengths, then I . . .

When I identify the values underlying challenges in my life, then I . . .

In a real sense, each of these steps requires us to capitalize on our strengths. It is what Grove and Glasser (2007) aptly call our *inner wealth*. They describe it as the steps that we proactively take to understand, acknowledge, and draw from our strengths to make positive choices. Figure 2.2 shows what a deficit-based versus a strengths-based approach looks like in practice. As we can see, a deficit-based system is a closed one. It shuts the door on the positive possibilities that can occur, whereas a strengths-based approach frees us to make choices that can improve our chances of success in achieving a positive goal.

When we are more prepared to work from our strengths, we are positioned more positively to work with our students. The strategies, approaches, and interventions provided throughout the remainder of this chapter are intended to help us better prepare to use a strengths-based approach with our students on a consistent, reliable, and predictable basis. This is particularly important

Figure 2.2 | **Example of Deficit-Based and Asset-Based Thinking**

A student transfers to my classroom midyear with a record of disruptive behaviors and well below grade-level academic skills.

Asset-Based Thinking

I have gone through similar situations before, and I reached out to good colleagues for support. I'm a collaborator, and I care deeply about my students. I am also good at establishing positive relationships with my students and earning their respect. Because I enjoy meeting new people, particularly those who are from diverse backgrounds, I would initiate a home visit to welcome this family to the school community.

Deficit-Based Thinking

This student has low academic skills and poor behavior. She will disrupt my whole classroom environment and require an amount of academic support that I can't give her.

when working with our targeted student population, who, by the nature of their lived experiences, need us to remind them of their inherent value and individual qualities.

Teaching students who have been deeply hurt requires that we provide an environment not only where they feel safe, but also where they experience a real sense of belonging, of being competent, and of being valued (Grove & Glasser, 2007). Let's explore these four essentials through the lens of Kelley Brown, a secondary classroom teacher.

 Take a Closer Look: Considering the Four Essentials Through a Teacher's Lens

Kelley Brown is a high school history teacher in Easthampton, Massachusetts. In addressing the topic of unconditional acceptance, she shares the following with us. As you will see, she has learned the genuine importance of caring for and caring about her students.

> It should not matter how a student responds to me. It is not per-
> sonal. If a student yells, swears, or cries, it is important to not respond
> with aggressive or abusive behavior. If I am caught in the moment
> and I cannot control myself, then I "tap out." No matter how much a
> student pushes me away, he has to know that I still care and that the
> relationship we have is not dictated by his emotional reaction.

As educators, our unconditional acceptance carries a message of *belonging* and emotional *safety*. It communicates, in words and deeds, that the student is welcome regardless of his background or current situation and is part of the fabric of the classroom and school.

It is also essential that our students experience a sense of feeling competent in our classrooms and schools. The message of *competency* is the affirmation that the student has what it takes to learn and to create positive relationships with others. It is the assurance that she has the ability to exert self-control and create positive outcomes. Kelley states the following:

> Every student enters the classroom with assets—the key is identi-
> fying them and helping students identify their own assets.

Kelley also mentions that finding the assets in all of our students can be challenging, as it will seem easier to do with some students than with others:

> Every student enters the classroom with assets and skills—some
> are more recognized than others, and some students are more often
> recognized as having assets than others. My job is to figure out those
> assets and help students see them as assets.

Lastly, but no less important, is the communication of human *value* to our students. Communicating human value is about allowing students to see how much their ideas, opinions, feelings, and full existence matter to their teachers and other adults in the school. It is also about demonstrating to them how worthy they are of others' respect, energy, time, kindness, and so on, all because they matters to their teachers and to others.

The following example of this type of demonstration that illuminates students' assets is Michael Silverstone's recounting of the importance of what he did to support a student to feel valued and competent.

Take a Closer Look: Making Our Students Feel Valued and Competent

Michael Silverstone is a veteran 2nd grade teacher in Massachusetts. He recounts an experience of what he did to support a student to feel valued and competent:

> I remember a boy who desperately resisted school structure, either avoiding work or acting miserable much of the time, but who found relief in drawing and tracing animals. He once gave me one of the pictures he had made on tracing paper, and I put it in a frame and placed it on top of a bookshelf in a prominent place in the classroom, where other students were able to see and compliment him on it. The fact that he was being recognized for an accomplishment that was on his own terms seemed to give him another way to think about school and opened the possibility for a successful experience in it.

A first step for illuminating students' assets is to know who they are. If we are to use our When . . . Then . . . construct, it would state, "When I know my students, then I am far more able to build an asset-based instructional program that is tailored to their personal, cultural, social, economic, linguistic, world, and academic experiences." Consequently, having a depth of understanding about our students and their families is a prerequisite for adopting a strengths-based perspective. It supplies us with the foundation that we need to build strong connections with our students and their families.

Take a Closer Look: Getting to Know Our Students to Appreciate Their Hidden Strengths

Creating strong connections with students who live with trauma, violence, and chronic stress may sound almost impossible, particularly because these students' overt behavior may push most of us away. It is when we summon the courage to get closer to them in a nonjudgmental manner that we learn about their many assets and strengths. Let's look at the following story from Marvin Quiñones, a high school teacher in Massachusetts, who at the time was in charge of a classroom created to provide an alternative to school suspension. Marvin was raised in the same neighborhood where the school was located and shared the same ethnicity as 95 percent of the students attending this high school.

Elias Santiago's life was cut short in 2013 at the age of 20. He died in a shootout that took place near my paternal grandmother's apartment. I used to look back fondly on the area, reminiscing about my memories of playing there as a child. Now that memory is tainted by the void created by my student's homicide. I remember the reactions of other educators who expressed their lack of surprise when hearing the news. Many of them said things like, "I saw that coming" or "He shouldn't have been there." However, many of them failed to realize that "there" was in fact his home. When I worked with Elias, I was mindful of the environment he spent his time in, because I had survived it. "Survived" being the operative word.

Elias had the reputation of being a "frequent flier" in our school. He spent a lot of time in internal suspension and, as a result, people assumed the worst of the young man. However, while Elias might have presented as the stereotypical stubborn inner-city student, our interactions demonstrated something much more profound than that label. The first thing I noticed about Elias was his command of the Spanish language. Amid lively conversation, his language swayed between the world of urban slang and something akin to the Chilean poet Pablo Neruda. This was one of the first innate strengths of Elias that I noticed.

Empathy came naturally to this young man. Although he was incessantly searching for a reason to get booted from his regular classes, he would often bring attention to things that he found unjust. He spared no one. He seemed to hold his friends and educators to the same accountability. He had a good moral compass and often asked for advice or critiques regarding decisions he had made; this compass seemed to defy the ongoing development of his prefrontal cortex.

In the interactions that I witnessed, Elias always seemed to be respectful and appreciative of women. He often spoke about his crush and how he had aspirations to provide for her one day. He seemed to have painted a picture of the future that he wanted. Most students, some who lived in environments less violent and chaotic than this young man, could not articulate their aspirations this readily. While the clear articulation of his aspirations was impressive, what was most admirable was his hunger for knowledge.

Elias noticed a tattoo I had of our indigenous ancestors in Puerto Rico: the Taino people of Boriken. He was so intrigued by what had motivated me to get the tattoo that the past, present, and future of Puerto Rico became an everyday topic of conversation for us. Learning about the independence movement on our island became the spark we had been searching for.

I remember the end of summer coming. I was excited to reconnect with the young man and urge him to recognize the strengths he possessed. Two weeks into that school year, I learned about his shooting. "A wasted life" is an understatement. Elias had strengths and resiliency within him. What he needed most was a patient, attentive mentor who would be present with him in realizing his talents.

There are many young people out there just like him. They need us the most. It's time that we make the locating and utilizing of these strengths and assets a priority for any adult working with young people. We need their stories to end differently.

There is no doubt this is a very compelling story, and its unfortunate and tragic ending should be a wake-up call and motivation for all of us as educators to genuinely adopt an asset-based perspective in our interactions with our students and others. Marvin Quiñones took the time to pay close attention to Elias's words and actions and looked beyond the evident behavior to find the goodness inside him. We should never underestimate the importance of building positive relationships, seeing beyond what could be perceived as deficits, and recognizing and acknowledging individuals' strengths and assets.

Preparing for a Strengths-Based Approach with Students

A big part of what we do is recognizing the effect that we can have on our students. John Hattie (2008) completed the largest meta-analyses of the key factors that affect student achievement, and of the 138 influencers that he examined, teacher relationships and feedback ranked among the top 8 percent. If we look closely at what this means in terms of our work with students living with trauma, violence, and chronic stress, we can see that the power of our influence in our interactions with students and the methods that we use have a great deal of significance for student outcomes. The importance of teacher-student relationships cannot be minimized, as these relationships have a great deal of influence on outcomes.

Hattie uses the concept of *mind frames* to describe the thinking that we must do to prepare and to teach. One of his critical findings is that it is our role to build and sustain positive relationships with our students. A second finding is that the feedback that we provide students is critical. These two ideas call for us to take time to learn about each of our students and build instructional programming based on our depth of knowledge about their personal, cultural, social, world, and academic experiences. In this way, we use the strengths that we have identified about ourselves to teach. In addition, we prepare to teach by first finding our students' strengths. Doing this requires that we build a foundation of trust in which students can count on our positive relationship with them. In addition to helping students see their own strengths, we must also help them in finding the strengths in others. Our work as teachers depends on us taking these actions. The formula in Figure 2.3 shows what we mean.

Building Relationships

Hattie's meta-analyses about the significance of relationships are bolstered by the more recent findings of renowned sociologist Joyce Epstein (2011). Her research shows a connection between the relationships that we build as

Figure 2.3 | Formula for a Strengths-Based Approach

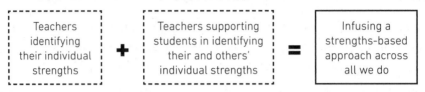

educators and the powerful gains that can be made by the students we teach. The process of building relationships is twofold:

1. Support students' understanding, acknowledgment, and validation of the strengths that they bring to the learning environment. This is what Grove and Glasser (2007) refer to as students' inner wealth.

2. Build relationships and an instructional program that is based on the foundation of our students' strengths.

Relationships require that we partner with people. They require us to engage with others through interactions. A strengths-based approach occurs through our continuously acknowledging and valuing students' strengths and building from these to support their learning through interaction. Helping these students create their personal asset-based account will greatly change the way they see themselves and interact with others. It is about learning to recognize goodness and values in themselves and others that otherwise go unnoticed or are buried under adversity.

Developing a keen ability to look for our students' assets requires us to pay close attention to minor behaviors that lead to successful outcomes. And when we do this, "we fearlessly, relentlessly pursue evidence with which to validate qualities of inner wealth" (Grove & Glasser, 2007, p. 66). We find evidence of inner wealth "in what students do; in what they *don't;* and in their intentions, hopes, successes, and even failures" (Grove & Glasser, 2007, p. 66). Sometimes it may take us breaking down simple routine activities to realize the many opportunities available to us to recognize and acknowledge hidden values, qualities, and strengths in others. Let's take, for example, a student who takes out her notepad, notebook, or tablet as requested. In order for her to do this, she initially had to make sure she put it in her bag after she used it the day before. She had to remember to bring it with her when she left for school that morning. She had to be tuned in and focused on what was happening in the classroom and paying attention to what the teacher requested. This student is being attentive, responsive, responsible, connected, and demonstrating her interest in learning.

This is the concept of creating *miracles from molecules* (Glasser, 2011). Following this mindset, the teacher recognizes the student's successes during this brief moment and reflects them back to her. The teacher then helps the student create a personal asset-based account. In Glasser's (2011) words, this is a "virtual place where we keep all our thoughts, ideas, judgments, and feelings about ourselves: who we are, what our value is to the world and how we think others see us" (p. 67). In other words, the way we communicate with our students, what we communicate to them, and our interactions with them create the experiences that will contribute to the students' portfolios. This place in their minds has the potential to be filled with reflections of students' greatness and a clear message of their inherent value as people. It is from this state of mind that students learn to capitalize on their own strengths and assets.

Let's look at a story of a student to see what we mean about the importance of helping students find or see their own strengths.

Michael is a 7th grade student who has been in the foster care system since he was 5 years old. He is now living in his fifth foster home. His attendance has been an issue throughout the years. His math skills are considered to be his relative academic strength. Teachers have noticed that he shows difficulty relating to and working with others. Specifically, Michael tends to take a long time joining the group and delays his participation in it. His teacher has been intentionally creating opportunities for Michael to demonstrate positive interactions with his classmates. Today, when the class separated into groups of five to solve several math problems, Michael went straight to his group and took his seat. How can the teacher take this moment, dissect it, and recognize the positive behaviors that led to Michael's reaction? What qualities and values did Michael clearly demonstrate? What evidence can the teacher use to validate Michael's inner wealth?

Using an asset-based perspective, the teacher promptly responded by reflecting back to Michael and giving him direct verbal feedback on the way he demonstrated cooperation and interest in engaging in the assigned activity. The teacher also energized Michael by describing to him how conscientious he had been about making good use of time (he physically directed himself to the location without taking extra time). Unlike in the past, he didn't wander off or ask to go to the bathroom. Rather, he went straight to the group. The teacher described to Michael that it was evident he was committed to his group and wanted the group to use time wisely. Michael also received affirmation from the teacher that he clearly chose what was important and showed great respect for his classmates who wanted to work on the assignment. Another quality that his teacher was able to bring to Michael's awareness was that he also showed wisdom and cooperation in making the choice that he knew was going to benefit the group.

Reflecting our students' strengths and assets is essential to help them become aware of their assets and to build their inner wealth. Students who live in traumatic, violent, and toxically stressful situations are less likely to receive the kind of feedback that would increase their awareness of all the goodness that exists inside them. As significant adults in their lives, we educators have the tremendous opportunity to change that by helping them build their personal asset-based accounts. The way we communicate and what we communicate to our students and adult peers has an effect on this process.

The following examples demonstrate the range of different activities that we can engage in to build relationships with our students. These activities also create opportunities for our targeted students to feel safe, to have a sense of belonging, and to feel competent and valued in our classrooms and schools. They are intended for the beginning of the school year or when new students enroll. Each example is followed by an activity to help you reflect on the example and apply each to your particular context.

Take a Closer Look: Getting to Know Our Young Learners to Identify Their Strengths

We have found it helpful to ask young learners to reflect on the following prompt and to ask them to write or draw a response. For example, kindergarten students can draw a picture and later label it with the support of their teacher. Students in grades 1–2 can write a few sentences and draw a picture. Teachers of students in grades 3–5 can expand the prompt to include "10 things that I wish my teacher knew about me."

What I Wish My Teacher Knew About Me

I wish my teacher knew that . . .

We can gain valuable insights about our students that we might otherwise have missed. For example, here are some statements that children wrote in response to the prompt:

- "Sometimes my papers are not signed because my mother isn't home a lot."
- "I can't fall asleep at night."
- "I feel like the class picks on me. I hate that."
- "I miss my dad. He got deported to Guatemala when I was 5 years old."
- "I don't have pencils to do my homework."
- "I don't want anyone to know that my mother is dying."

As asset-based people, we are now capable of finding personal qualities and values even in situations where we may see none at first glance. Take, for example, this student response: "Sometimes my papers are not signed because my mother isn't home a lot." What we see is that this student values responsibility because he wants to bring the papers signed, as his teacher has requested. He is very honest and doesn't try to tell a lie even if it feels embarrassing to tell the truth. He has integrity; he wants to do the right thing and wants the teacher to know what may be in the way of doing it. And, of course, he values education because he cares about meeting his responsibilities as a student.

 Time for Reflection

Following a strengths-based approach, find the personal values and qualities demonstrated by the young learners' statements you just read in response to the prompt "I wish my teacher knew that . . ."

 Take a Closer Look: Getting to Know Our Middle and High School Students to Identify Their Strengths

Part of our quest as educators is to support students in becoming part of their school community and beyond. Keith Malletta, a high school English teacher in North Carolina, helps students become active members of his classroom and community by engaging in the following activity on the first day of class. He gives an index card to each of his students. On the front of the card, he asks them to write their name and nickname. On the back of the card, he asks them to respond to the following prompts:

- Activities that you are involved in at our high school.
- Activities that you are involved in outside of school.
- Activities that you do at home.

Keith shares his reasons for engaging students in this activity. He says that the students who do not respond to the prompts by leaving any one of them blank are the first ones he builds relationships with. He dedicates time to finding out their interests and works to support their involvement in activities that match these. For example, Keith encourages students to become members of various after-school clubs.

 Time for Reflection

1. Consider the questions that Keith asks of his students. In what ways do you believe that these support him in building relationships with his students and students in building relationships with others in their community?

2. In what ways do you believe that this activity supports Keith in building a classroom environment where students feel valued, feel competent, and have a sense of belonging?

3. What obstacles do you envision might occur using all of the strategies discussed for young learners and secondary learners? What would you do and who would you work with to ensure that these obstacles are removed and converted into strengths?

 Take a Closer Look: Additional Ways for Getting to Know Our Older Students and Find Their Strengths

Keith also asks students to rate themselves in a variety of ways. As you read each of the following items, consider its purpose in terms of finding the strengths and assets that all students possess. Keith's entire focus is that students already are, and will become more, promising editors, writers, readers, and communicators and will build stronger capacities to get along with others.

- Rate yourself on a scale of 1–5 (5 is the strongest) as an editor.
- Rate yourself on a scale of 1–5 (5 is the strongest) as a writer.
- Rate yourself on a scale of 1–5 (5 is the strongest) as a reader.
- Rate yourself on a scale of 1–5 (5 is the strongest) as a communicator.
- Rate on a scale of 1–5 (5 is the strongest) your ability to get along with others.

Time for Reflection

How might students' responses provide opportunities for Keith to reflect on all of the greatness that students exhibit in each of these areas?

All the activities presented thus far in this chapter reflect a culture of caring and empathy for ourselves and for others. They also reflect the promising practice of engaging with students in positive ways. This shift toward positivity positions us in two ways. First, we believe that all students can learn and be members of our learning communities. Second, we believe that this will occur. A challenge for many of us working in increasingly diverse classroom settings with students living with trauma, violence, and chronic stress is that we might not have the familiarity needed to truly know that we have created a culture of caring and empathy. An important first step toward gaining this familiarity is to learn about our students. Keith shows us how he does it, but there are many additional ways for doing this.

Educational scholar Brendalyn Tosolt (2009) helps us understand the importance of students' perceptions of their teachers' caring and empathy, particularly as applied to diverse student populations that experience trauma, violence, and chronic stress. One of her important findings about students from diverse populations is that they perceive caring and empathy differently. Securing information from a student about the types of caring that are important has been found to greatly help in the quest to build strong and lasting relationships. The survey questionnaire in Figure 2.4 has been adapted from Tosolt (as cited in Zacarian & Silverstone, 2015). Students are given the survey early in the school year and are asked to check the box that most applies.

Figure 2.4 | Types of Teacher Caring

	Types of Caring from Teacher	Very Important	Important	Not Very Important
1.	Admits that he or she is wrong sometimes			
2.	Helps me when other kids are picking on me			
3.	Helps me with a problem not related to school			
4.	Smiles at me			
5.	Protects me			
6.	Listens to my side of the story			
7.	Gets involved when other students are being mean to each other			
8.	Writes helpful comments on my writing			
9.	Lets me ask lots of questions			
10.	Holds classroom discussions that encourage a lot of student talk			
11.	Holds me accountable for my schoolwork			
12.	Is known (by prior students and for years) to care about students			
13.	Has ongoing relationships with students and families outside of school			
14.	Offers support after school and/or during the summer months			
15.	Is curious about me			
16.	Enjoys teaching			
17.	Makes an effort to make school meaningful			
18.	Makes an effort to make classroom life enjoyable on a regular basis			
19.	Cares about the subject(s) he or she teaches and wants me to have access to it in a generous way			

Source: Adapted from Tosolt (2008).

Let's look at how this questionnaire might be used in practice to acknowledge a student's sense of belonging, of being competent, and of being valued and feeling safe in our classrooms and schools. Wanda Ortiz uses the questionnaire on the first day of school and, upon reviewing it, notes that Joey's response to statement #9 is that it is very important for him when his teacher "lets me ask a lot of questions." This is an opportunity for Wanda to see how Joey values learning when he works with a teacher who welcomes his curiosity, willingness to learn, and contributions to classroom discussions.

 ## Time for Reflection

Select three statements about teacher caring from Figure 2.4. Describe how this activity can contribute to creating a classroom where students feel they belong, feel valued and competent, and feel safe.

 ## Take a Closer Look: Involving Students in Creating a Classroom That Showcases the Four Essentials

Let's go back to Kelley Brown, the high school U.S. history teacher in a small, old, industrial community in a rural area of Massachusetts. She routinely asks her students, "What do I do that keeps you interested in learning?" Her students write a note in response to this question to let Kelley know their thoughts. When any student lets Kelley know, as any student can, that what she is doing is not working (e.g., I am bored, I don't like this lesson, I don't understand), Kelley then asks them what they suggest she can do to make learning more engaging and what she can do to support her students in their personal lives. This activity can be adapted for students in K–12.

Time for Reflection

What are two or three additional questions that teachers might ask their students to make learning more engaging and to show students that they are safe, valued, and competent and belong to their classroom?

Taking time to engage in the preparatory steps discussed in this chapter helps us greatly to work with students and families living with trauma, violence, and chronic stress by using an asset-based approach and seeing the abundant internal strengths that students possess and which they can draw from and rely on. The next chapter will explore how we can create a strengths-based classroom environment where all students can learn.

Creating a Strengths-Based Classroom Learning Environment

The curriculum of teaching students that they are good and valuable people is the most lasting lesson a teacher can ever teach.

—Tom Grove and Howard Glasser,
The Inner Wealth Initiative

Chapter 2 looked at the preparatory steps educators must take to use an asset-based approach with students living with trauma, violence, and chronic stress. It showed the critical importance of identifying the positive and inherent qualities and values in our students and their families to build trusting relationships. Chapter 3 shows how we can apply this approach to the classroom so that students living with trauma, violence, and chronic stress experience a real sense of belonging, of being competent, of being valued, and of feeling safe (Grove & Glasser, 2007). We consider these four essentials to be the basis for creating an asset-based classroom that is inclusive and responsive to students living with adversity. This chapter examines the following:

- Creating a physical environment that respects students' learning preferences and is conducive for learning.

- Building positive, asset-based student-teacher relationships in the classroom.
- Fostering student engagement by promoting student voice and choice.
- Establishing predictable routines and a gradual release of responsibility to foster students' strengths.

Creating a Physical Environment That Respects Students' Learning Preferences and Is Conducive for Learning

Learning spaces have the ability to positively or negatively affect students' learning and morale. As Denise Young (2002), from the School of Education at the University of North Carolina, states, the classroom is a "home away from home" for you and the students. From the arrangement of desks to what we choose to place on the classroom walls, every detail counts toward our efforts to keep students engaged and maximize cooperation and creativity. The classroom should be an environment that facilitates and reinforces the skills necessary to be successful in a global society that demands constant communication, collaboration, teamwork, and innovation. In addition, it is particularly important for our students who live with trauma, violence, and chronic stress to learn in an environment that fosters a sense of belonging and of feeling valued, competent, and safe. To minimize the adverse effects of physical and environmental factors on the learning disposition of all of our students, consider the following:

1. Seating arrangements should be conducive for collaboration, open discussion, and teamwork, and there should be areas that welcome individual work, mental concentration, and focus while diminishing distractibility.

2. Place important daily lesson details in an area that has been agreed on by all and is visually accessible to everyone in the classroom.

3. Environmental factors such as lighting, air quality, and acoustics should help students feel comfortable and ready to learn. Although we may encounter financial challenges to addressing these factors, changes that require minimum investment (e.g., adding a floor or desk lamp in a corner designed for reading, if fire regulations permit; having plants that add aesthetics and, in some cases, healthier air quality) may make a significant positive difference.

Building Positive, Asset-Based Student-Teacher Relationships in the Classroom

Chapter 2 introduced strategies for building trusting relationships with our students. Let's look at some actions we should take to build those relationships.

Identify and Acknowledge Students' Strengths and Assets

We can use many strategies to identify the strengths and assets of students living with trauma, violence, and chronic stress. For example, in Chapter 2 we met Keith Malletta, a high school English teacher. We showed the steps that he takes to get to know his students. If you recall, the very first day that students arrive in his classroom, whether at the beginning of the semester or during the school year, he gives them an index card and has them write their name and nickname on the front of the card and respond to a series of questions on the back about activities they are involved in. (This activity can be modified for students who prefer to speak their answers.)

An important goal from the very beginning of our work with students should be identifying their strengths and assets, in the form of values and qualities, and reflecting these back to our students. For example, Keith asks students about the activities they are involved in outside of school. He uses this information to make a positive statement about what he learns: "You work so hard in school, and you have an after-school job as well. I am inspired by your determination and your ability to manage responsibilities!"

Our goal is to continuously gather as much information as we can about our students' strengths and assets so that we can build and strengthen our relationships with them by personalizing our interactions. It is not rare to hear Keith building on what he learns. Here is an example of what he might say to continuously engage students in activities, showing that he is deepening his understanding of and relationship with his students: "Good morning, Lilliana. Great to see you after that rough game last night. I heard you were very determined on that court!"

Chapter 2 also provided an activity for young students titled "What I Wish My Teacher Knew About Me." Activities such as this help build relationships with all of our students, including those living with trauma, violence, and chronic stress. They also provide us with information about our students' strengths so that we may connect these to our instruction in order to make learning more relevant and meaningful for our students. Later in the chapter, we'll see how some teachers do this.

As educators who usually follow a tight daily schedule to fit in all that we need to teach, we may question how and when we are going to be able to engage in such interactions. One practical and beneficial way is to greet students as they enter the classroom. We can use this moment to address our students with a positive and welcoming greeting that acknowledges them by name and includes a message about the assets and strengths that we have identified and the ones we continue to learn from them.

 Time for Reflection

Create one or two additional activities that you could implement to welcome students and use the power of your asset-based language to acknowledge them while reflecting back their value or quality.

Continuously Observe Students Living with Trauma, Violence, and Chronic Stress Through an Asset-Based Lens

We build students' sense of belonging, of being competent, of being valued, and of feeling safe from the start when we intentionally look for underlying individual values and attributes in students' behaviors. What is key is to help students feel accepted for exactly who they are and what they bring to our classroom communities. Let's look at an example of what we mean. It comes from Chris Homiak, a middle school English and mathematics teacher of English learners in Kansas City, Missouri. He tells us about Javier, a 7th grade student.

Take a Closer Look: Finding a Student's Strengths

Javier was a gift to us. An English learner whose home language is Spanish, he joined our 7th grade class after being out of school for six months. Prior to enrolling in our school, he had recently moved across the country and was in transition, living in homeless shelters with his large family.

At first, Javier answered questions very quietly, and his eyes often looked toward the floor or quickly around the room. Also, he often got out of his seat without permission and walked in a small circle near his desk.

Time for Reflection

Pretend you are Mr. Homiak.

1. What values and attributes does Javier possess that stopped him from making poor choices?

2. Make a list of Javier's attributes. What would you say to Javier to acknowledge what you have identified? Make sure you label the values so Javier can incorporate them into his personal account of strengths.

Chapter 2 introduced the concept of having attributes that often stop us from making bigger mistakes or poor choices. It is important to mention this again because we all need to work on developing the ability to look for values in behaviors that may seem, at first glance, to be negative. Take, for example, this section of Javier's story: *Also, he often got out of his seat without permission and walked in a small circle near his desk.* At first glance, getting out of his seat without permission may seem to be an unacceptable behavior and, indeed, difficult to view as an asset. As discussed in earlier chapters, adopting an asset-based perspective requires us to find evidence "in what students do; in what they *don't;* and in their intentions, hopes, successes, and even failures" (Grove & Glasser, 2007, p. 66). In this example, Javier didn't disrupt class by yelling or screaming, or by going to other students to talk to them. He contained himself in a small area, trying not to disrupt the class. This is the behavior we focus on, and the one that we want to acknowledge and reflect back to him to make it visible and transparent. The goal is for Javier to see his strengths, value his own self-worth, create a personal account of his strengths, and begin to operate by drawing from it. Among Javier's assets is his ability to understand what he needs to turn his classroom environment into a favorable learning experience for him. In this case, it is an environment that will allow him the opportunity to engage in movement like standing, stretching, and moving his body. (Think of yourself during those long professional development trainings!) It is also evidence of Javier's good judgment, consideration, and respect for other people's spaces and time for learning because his behavior is contained and not disruptive.

Support Students to Acknowledge and Draw from Their Strengths

Thus, as important as it is to acknowledge students' strengths, it is equally important to make these known to students so that they may create a self-image based on these strengths, draw confidence from them, and use what Grove and Glasser (2007) call students' *inner wealth* to succeed in their classroom communities and beyond. The following are two examples of what different teachers have done to help their students develop these assets. The first example shows what teacher Chris Homiak did to support Javier in seeing his strengths. The second presents what Tina Kern, a high school ESL teacher in New Jersey, did to support her student to do the same.

Take a Closer Look: Making Strengths Visible and Transparent

Observing Javier during independent work time, I saw that he had a deep capacity for abstract thinking and that he was strong in algebra. I shared my observation by saying, "Javier, you are such a strong problem solver and algebra thinker! I noticed that you can see patterns and break down the parts until you solve the problem." As his trusting relationships grew in our small group, I pushed him to explain his answers in more detail and to explore alternative ways for solving the same problem. Initially, he wanted to share his answers first and fast; I supported him to wait for others to catch up and to see if he could help find their mistakes. I often turned to him to provide constructive feedback or error correction, handing over the document camera or whiteboard for him to play the teacher role.

Time for Reflection

Pretend you are Chris Homiak.

1. What underlying values or qualities can you identify in Javier's behavior?

2. Make a list of Javier's attributes. What would you say to Javier to acknowledge the attributes you have identified? Make sure you label the
values so he can incorporate them into his personal account of assets.

In this example, teacher Chris Homiak sees that Javier has strengths in
abstract thinking and algebra. He does more than acknowledge these strengths;
he makes them visible and transparent to Javier and capitalizes on them by
showing Javier as a contributing leader in the class. Let's take a look at high
school teacher Tina Kern in our second example.

Take a Closer Look: Making Strengths Visible and Transparent

As I scanned the class the first day of school, I saw Ana, a small
young girl, sitting alone clutching her new school-issued tablet like
a shield. When I looked at her, she seemed to visibly flinch and draw
herself tighter against the wall. I thought to myself how brave she
was. She exhibited such courage and resilience by coming to a new
school where she didn't have any friends yet and didn't speak the
same language as her classmates.

I told her that I thought she was brave to leave her country and
make the arduous trip to the United States. She was brave to come
to school where she knew no one. My reward was a little smile, and
soon there was a fissure in the barrier.

I still remember vividly when Ana produced a sentence in English.
There was silence—and then the students applauded. We did it
together!

Use Positive Language with Others Working in Our Classrooms

As important as it is to use positive energy and positive, asset-based language, we want to ensure that all who work with us in our classrooms do the same. We include specialists, aides, and others who work with us on behalf of student learning and membership in our classrooms. Let's look at two hypothetical examples. In each, a teacher describes her work with a particular student to a person who works in her classroom.

Example 1: Lisette, "The Difficult Student"

Good luck working with Lisette. Her home life is terrible. Her parents are always fighting with each other and are getting a divorce. Lisette is a real challenge in my classroom. She picks fights with other students, and I hate it when I have to put her in a group because I can never trust her to get along with others.

Example 2: Lisette, "The Student I Love to Teach"

Lisette is a new student in our classroom. While her prior teacher tells us that her parents were divorcing and that there was a lot of stress at home, she is a resilient individual. I think she endured a lot last year with her parents' divorce and still managed to show up to school and make the best of her day. I observe her taking care of her siblings when they come to school in the morning, showing love and responsibility. I like the way she volunteers an answer in our science classes, showing her curiosity and knowledge. She loves science! When we did a unit of study on microscopes, she helped the class set up the microscopes and loved sharing what she saw on the slides. I intentionally partner her with students who have had little experience or desire to use a microscope. They find Lisette's enthusiasm to be contagious. She's a great asset in my class!

Time for Reflection

Consider the two examples and complete the following questions.

1. Our energy and relationships with students are considered to be our biggest asset, or "prize," in working with them. Compare where these two teachers are placing their energy when working with Lisette. Discuss two or three differences that you notice. Be as specific as possible.

2. What assets, in terms of qualities and values, do you see in Lisette as described in example 2?

Fostering Student Engagement by Promoting Student Voice and Choice

Individuals who live in traumatic situations are likely to experience a complete loss of control and sense of powerlessness. As such, regaining control is crucial to coping with traumatic stressors (Perry & Szalavitz, 2006). In the classroom, this translates to implementing practices that value and encourage students' participation in decisions that matter to them. The end result of this practice is students who feel empowered and in control of their lives.

Student empowerment is defined as "giving young people the opportunity to actively participate in school activities and decisions that will shape their lives, the lives of their families and the lives of their peers" (Mind Matters, n.d.). Classroom environments that promote empowerment do so by building students' confidence and capacity to speak up, present and address issues of their concern, make changes, and take risks. Students are more likely to encounter success in this process when adults become partners and provide active support. Toshalis and Nakkula conceptualize student voice as "the antithesis of depersonalized, standardized, and homogenized educational experiences because it begins and ends with the thoughts, feelings, visions, and actions of the students themselves . . . this makes student voice profoundly student centered" (2012, p. 23). This gives our students living with trauma, violence, and chronic stress a sense of competency and of being valued, which is observable in both of the examples that we drew from teachers Chris Homiak and Tina Kern.

Our next example is from Larry Ferlazzo, an inner-city high school teacher from California, well-known author, and educational leader. He recounts an occurrence in his history class where he combined his understanding of the trauma that his students experienced with his knowledge of their cultures and backgrounds, as well as how he built an effective lesson around his students' assets by using a fully student-centered learning experience. As we will see, Larry was not sure if his selections were "too close to home" for his students. Drawing from the lessons he learned from engaging students in this experience, he makes some critical suggestions for enabling students' voice and choice, as well as ownership of their learning.

 Take a Closer Look: Using Connections from Students' Lives to Support Learning

I've taught many students, both immigrants and non-immigrants, who either have experienced or are continuing to experience trauma. Building a relationship with these students is key to forming a cohesive classroom. The key strategy that I use is to be supportive, particularly by emphasizing two-way conversation as opposed to one-way communication.

Here's one example from this past semester. The majority of students in my class were refugees from Central America, many of whom experienced major traumatic events in their home countries and on their journey to the United States.

When I wanted to introduce my students to a first-person account about gang violence in El Salvador, I had conversations with them to see how they would feel reading such a piece in class, whether it would hit "too close to home." All of them said they wanted to read it, but when I brought copies to class, one student, Alfredo, said he wanted to read it alone in the corner. Alfredo took his copy of the article, moved his desk to one of the corners, and positioned it so he had his back to the rest of us.

The rest of the class began reading the piece together, with students leaping at the chance to interject their own comments and connections. At one point, I could tell, even from just seeing his back, that Alfredo was having a hard time. When I walked over to him, he took out his phone and began to show me photographs of all his friends who had been killed by gang violence in El Salvador and told me their stories.

Afterward, all of the students, including Alfredo (who had previously not been very interested in academic work), asked that we read and write as much as possible about what was happening in Central America.

I was able to form a more interconnected classroom community and provide opportunities for highly engaging academic lessons through the following:

1. Respecting students by asking their permission to bring in an article on such a personal "hot-button" issue.

2. Acknowledging the different ways they might want to react to it.

3. Listening to their personal commentaries.

Leading with our ears instead of our mouths works with students experiencing trauma—and with most others, too!

Time for Reflection

1. Larry Ferlazzo suggests that we acknowledge the different ways that students might react to literature, a news report, or other piece of writing. How might you construct this idea in a classroom setting?

2. One of Larry's suggestions is "leading with our ears instead of our mouths." Describe two or three ways that you might do this to ensure students' voices are heard.

3. Think of the many ways you can encourage student voice and choice and foster a sense of empowerment in your students. Describe one way you can begin to incorporate these two concepts in your classroom.

Connecting Content to Students' Lives and Experiences

Engagement consists of three components: affect, cognition, and behavior (Yonezawa & Jones, 2009). In order for engagement to occur in our students' learning experience, Quaglia and Corso (2014) expand on the three conditions of engagement:

1. Fun and excitement that relates to students' emotional investment in what they are learning.

2. Curiosity and creativity that is connected to students' intellectual engagement in what they are learning.

3. Spirit of adventure that reflects students' willingness to engage in the behaviors necessary to learn. (p. 80)

While we might not consider school as being fun or exciting (as so much of what students do is tied to a standard, set curriculum, or test), a good deal of research points to the importance of providing lessons and instruction that get students excited about learning. A helpful way to think about it is to consider how we can foster learning to be socially and culturally relevant for students living with trauma, violence, and chronic stress. It is equally important to connect learning to what is relevant in our students' lives that builds from their personal, cultural, social, and world experiences. In describing this from a brain-based perspective, Hammond (2015) states that our positive energy and passion as teachers and the ways that we acknowledge students' background experiences supports the engagement of students' brains because it connects positive emotions with students' current levels of expertise and competencies.

When we have an understanding of our students' personal, cultural, social, and world experiences, we can connect these to the curriculum to be studied. Let's look at two examples from the field. Our first one revisits teacher Chris Homiak, and in our second we meet Kathy Lobo, an elementary school teacher in Massachusetts.

Take a Closer Look: Connecting Curriculum to Students' Interests

I push students to increase the quality and quantity of their academic English by using curriculum that is highly relevant to students' lives—ranging from video game addiction to girls playing on boys' sports teams, drug testing in schools, and junk food access.

Securing Literature and Examples That Support Students Living with Trauma, Violence, and Chronic Stress

As important as it is to try to connect learning to what we believe are students' interests, it is always helpful to secure literature and examples that are socially relevant to our students' experiences. Psychiatric specialists Everly and Firestone (2013) tell us the following:

> Do not underestimate the power of characters in literature as a means of addressing and diminishing and restoring of these beliefs. At the elementary, middle and high school levels these characters can be discussed in great length for their ambition to overcome challenges, their reliance (or lack of reliance) on support systems, on individual coping mechanisms and overall outcomes. (p. 291)

In this next example, Kathy Lobo shows the importance of finding literary characters that support students living with trauma, violence, and chronic stress in the ways that Everly and Firestone discuss.

Take a Closer Look: Connecting Literature to Students' Experiences

What I do to prepare for working with and supporting students who have experienced or are experiencing trauma, violence, or chronic stress that also draws from their strengths includes choosing books that teach about experiences and feelings that are universal to all. I try to choose novels and stories to read with the students that can inspire mini-lessons on topics relevant to things they are learning in their content-area classes.

For example, I chose to read the chapter book *Tornado* by Newbury Medal–winning author Betsy Byars. At the start of the book, there is a storm coming, and a mother, her two sons, and a hired farmhand named Pete hide in a shelter. While the tornado rages outside, Pete tells the boys a story from his youth. The story helps pass the time and also distract them from worrying about the father, who is outside in the storm. Pete tells how his family found a frightened dog in a doghouse after a similar storm had hit.

I have found that this story is engaging for students and can be a great starting point for teaching and building from their background experiences, including the notion of hiding and being safe from weather events and natural disasters or coping with fear and worry. Also, in the story Pete tells about playing cards, and that provides a context to talk about popular children's games. I have found this to be a helpful connection because across cultures some games have equivalents, like the game of jacks. One student shared that in Haiti they use some bones from goats to toss and catch. Another student from South Korea brought in plastic objects that look like nuts (as in nuts and bolts) that they use to play a similar game. I brought in some jacks from the United States, and we used a ball. The sharing of traditional games really motivates students to open up and share.

Chris Homiak's and Kathy Lobo's examples show us how they connected the content being studied with their students' personal, cultural, social, and world experiences. For example, Kathy's example helps students make connections between the experiences of literary characters and their own lives. It also allows them to see how others have dealt with the same emotions that they are experiencing.

Establishing Predictable Routines That Foster Students' Strengths

Clinical psychologist and director of the Trauma Training and Education Division at the Trauma Center at the Justice Resource Institute Margaret Blaustein

(2013) affirms what many teachers and specialists have found to be essential when working with students living with trauma, violence, and chronic stress. These include using routines and practices that are consistent and predictable. According to Blaustein, using the same routines and rituals in our classroom activities is critical because so many students who have been exposed to the unpredictable nature of trauma, violence, and chronic stress live with fear of uncertainty. A classroom environment that has a set of predictable routines, schedules, sequences, and practices allows such students to downshift from a fearful state where unpredictability takes control, to a calmer and more positive one where events happen in a predictable manner. Blaustein calls this creating a predictable rhythm to the students' day that they can count on. Expert psychologists Kilmer, Gil-Rivas, and Hardy (2013) echo Blaustein's emphasis on routines, especially for students who have experienced natural disasters and terrorism, as a critical means of helping students "reclaim normalcy" (p. 235).

Routines and Practices at Enrollment

At the beginning of the school year or at any time that students enroll in our school, we must let them know a range of important routine information that some of us may take for granted. The following questions help us clarify the routine responses that our students need:

- What time does school actually start, and when should students arrive?
- What should students do if there is a delayed opening or a school closing (e.g., due to inclement weather)?
- If there is a delay, should students go directly into the school or wait on the playground?
- Where should students go if they arrive at school late?
- Do students need to get a late pass?
- Where do students put their coats and backpacks when they enter their classroom? Where does their homework go?
- What should students be doing while they are waiting for the rest of the class to arrive?
- Who will be the teacher, and what's his or her name?

One of us once had a student, Mei, who came from China. On her first day, Mei came to school at 7:00 a.m., as that is the time school started in her hometown in China. She was found sitting in a dark classroom with her coat on when her classroom teacher arrived at 8:15 a.m. It was obvious that no one had thought to tell Mei's family what time school started!

Routines and Practices in the Classroom

It is also important to create and implement routines and practices to ensure that students living with trauma, violence, and chronic stress see and experience a familiar and predictable rhythm to their day. These include the ways in which we do the following:

- Start class.
- Start the lessons.
- Sequence the lessons.
- Transition students from one task to the next during our lessons.
- End the lessons.
- Support students during non-instructional activities.

Let's discuss some examples that teachers have found to be helpful for building routine practices. Young students often gather on a rug for what is commonly called "morning meeting" or "circle time." You may be familiar with this and can picture a group of learners seated on the classroom rug at the beginning of the school day, with their teacher seated at the front in a chair. A common morning meeting scenario looks something like this: Teachers welcome the whole group, followed by a few students sharing an experience from home by "showing and telling," followed by teachers doing a mini-lesson, and ending with them sharing the day's class schedule. These types of whole-class gatherings are appropriate for all grade levels when they are welcoming and highly predictable.

Here are some suggestions for these opening segments at the start of a school day, for elementary school students, and at the beginning of a class, for secondary students.

1. Welcome students using asset-based language that lets them know they are welcomed and valuable members of the classroom community.

2. Engage students in a sharing activity about special news, such as the arrival of a new sibling, an occasion such as a birthday, or a school event or sports, performance, or curricular activity. Create routines for this sharing activity to help it be a predictable social activity.

3. Provide information about the day or class schedule so that students know what to expect during the school day or class period.

4. Conduct a short academic or social learning experience. For example, during one meeting, a teacher asked for a student volunteer to share with the class the process that students should follow when leaving from and returning to the classroom for small-group instruction. His teaching goal was to support his students in making transitions and empower students in making good choices.

5. Support students to transition from the opening meeting to the next classroom activity by noticing and acknowledging those who show any sign of readiness.

The goal behind any routines we create is to establish predictability without being inflexible. For younger and older students alike, there needs to be a balance between activities where students can physically move around and those where they remain seated (Mahar et al., 2006). Behavioral specialists Hertel and Johnson (2013) amplify the importance of physical activity in our classrooms for students living with trauma, violence, and chronic stress. They stress the importance of routinely having students get up, move around, and engage in physical activity whenever possible. They provide examples of schools and classrooms that have built physical exercise, such as walking and gardening clubs and other physical activities, into the school day or classroom routines because of its critical role in healthy brain functioning and learning.

Routines and Practices Throughout the School Day

Students living with trauma, violence, and chronic stress, and their peers, also need to experience smooth transitions throughout the school day. For example, students who leave the classroom for small-group instruction (e.g., ESL class, speech and language therapy session, special education instruction, math or reading support) need to have a predictable routine so that their day has a rhythm and is as seamless as possible. Many students may not have small-group instruction at the same time every day. Indeed, many special area classes, speech and language sessions, and more may be held only once or twice per week. This reality makes for a morning/circle time meeting or start-of-class meeting all the more critical for making these schedules known.

The transition from one event to the next is also important to consider. Some elementary school teachers, for example, play soft music to indicate the transition between one subject matter and the next. While secondary schools typically have bells that signal the end of a class, it is also important to create transitions between each segment of our lessons and have an ending routine that occurs before the bell rings. An example is an "exit ticket" a few moments before the bell: The teacher asks a question to capture an important learning piece taught during the period, and students respond on the ticket and hand it to the teacher on their way out of the classroom.

Lessons with Predictable Routines

It is also critical to design and deliver lessons with predictable routines to ensure students living with trauma, violence, and chronic stress thrive in a learning environment where they feel safe, competent, valued, and a sense of belonging. First, we must incorporate the previously presented three elements of a strengths-based learning environment, which are illustrated in Figure 3.1.

In addition, we must do the following:

- Communicate and model our thinking and understanding of the subject matter and related skills to be learned.
- Give students multiple opportunities to engage with and practice using the language and skills of the subject matter to be learned.

Let's look at an example of a lesson from elementary school teacher Mark Zimmerman, adapted from Zacarian and Silverstone (2015) and Silverstone and Zacarian (2012), that incorporates all of these routines.

Figure 3.1 | Elements of a Strengths-Based Classroom Learning Environment

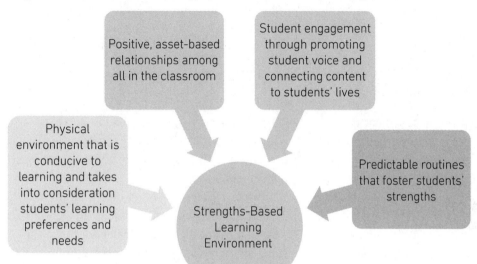

Take a Closer Look: Putting the Principles into Practice

As you read the description of this lesson, notice the routines and practices that are embedded in it and the steps Mark Zimmerman takes to best ensure that the lesson is relevant to his students' lives and draws from their strengths. In other words, how does he factor in the four elements needed for creating and implementing a strengths-based classroom environment? Let's look more closely.

Mark works in a heterogeneous class with students experiencing and not experiencing trauma, violence, and chronic stress; students learning English as a second language; students with identified learning disabilities; and students living in significant poverty. He is designing a lesson on odd and even numbers that is based on the routines that he generally uses. While he is using the textbook Investigations and is drawing from his district's and state's mathematics standards, he knows the importance of building connections between what is relevant to his students and the content to be learned. He observes that many of his students return to class very upset with what is occurring at recess. Some tell him that a classmate didn't "play fair," others report that a classmate was "too bossy," and others tell him that they felt "left out."

To activate his students' interest in learning the mathematics concepts and to provide students with the important voice and level of engagement that we have discussed, Mark poses a question to his students. First, he writes a learning objective on the whiteboard, followed with what they will learn that day. He takes a bunch of Popsicle sticks and labels each with a student's name. He also labels a stick with his name. Using an LCD camera that is projected onto a large screen in front of the class, he shows the students as he puts all the sticks in a can. He also prepares a list of the math vocabulary that students need to master (e.g., odd numbers, even numbers, pairs) and displays this on the whiteboard for all to see. He takes five sticks out of the can, including his own and, drawing his stick away from the rest, he asks students, "What does it feel like when I am the 'odd man out'?" He explains what this idiomatic expression means and discusses what it feels like for him when he is not included. He then asks students to go to their "learning stations," where they have organized their desks into small groups of four. He asks students to work with a "shoulder partner" to discuss solutions to the problem of participation that is occurring on the playground, connecting the content of mathematics with what is occurring at recess. He then asks that the pairs work with their small group to share their solutions using the mathematics vocabulary that he has posted on the whiteboard and to select the solutions they think are the most helpful.

Following the sequence of lesson routines that he always uses, Mark plans a lesson that has a rhythm that is familiar to his students because it occurs repeatedly in the classroom. He makes sure that students have multiple transition opportunities to physically get up and move around the classroom. To ensure that they stay on task, he reconnects students to the overarching unit objectives as well as the day's content learning objective and what they will do to learn at each transition. Figure 3.2 is an example of the routines and practices that occur in Mark's class. We can see that they involve six routine steps.

Figure 3.2 | Mr. Zimmerman's Routine Lesson Sequence

Step 1 Mr. Zimmerman a. Reviews overarching unit objective on *odd* and *even numbers.* b. Reviews day's learning objective and what students will do to learn concepts. c. Revisits the unit and day's learning objectives and what students will do to learn at each transition.	←	Step 2: Mr. Zimmerman thinks aloud and models the skills and activity students will do. Example: What does it feel like when you are the "odd man out"?
	←	Step 3: Students engage in pairs, finding solutions to being the odd man out at recess using math language.
	←	Step 4: Students engage in small groups, discussing solutions to being the odd man out using the language of math.
	←	Step 5: The whole class reviews paired and small-group activities and solutions and comes to agreement about them.
	←	Step 6: Students discuss the problem of participation at recess with a family member or friend and ask for additional suggestions for solutions.

Source: Adapted from Haynes and Zacarian (2010, p. 109).

 Time for Reflection

1. Drawing from Mark Zimmerman's plans, create an illustration of the routines that you would use to provide a predictable rhythm to your lessons.

2. Describe the sequence that you have created.

3. Describe what you did to incorporate the four elements of a strengths-based learning environment.

If we look closely at the steps that Mark uses to teach mathematics, we see that he initially provides direct, explicit instruction to his whole class, followed by students engaging in paired and then small-group tasks, discussing their work as a whole class, and ending with students going home and discussing what they are learning with a family member or a friend. The steps that he uses create a continuous rhythm that his students can count on and, at the same time, a high volume of student interactions and empowerment in their own learning.

Many might refer to the lesson that Mark taught as using a gradual release of responsibility (Pearson & Gallagher, 1983). While it is often referred to as an "I do it, we do it, you do it model" (Knost & Perry, 2016) that begins with explicit direct instruction, followed with guided practice, followed with activities that rely incrementally less and less on direct instruction, we might erroneously believe that the model initially involves too little student choice and active involvement. But when we look closely at what Mark did, we see that he engaged students in a high level of choice to collaboratively determine solutions to the problem they were experiencing at recess.

Figure 3.3 shows the steps of a gradual release of responsibility that we have drawn from Fisher and Frey (2013). It takes into account the same elements that Mark Zimmerman used and incorporates what we illustrated in Figure 3.1. We use it to show another example of a classroom teacher and her unit of study in language arts.

Figure 3.3 | Gradual Release of Responsibility

Components	Description	Examples
Physical environment is organized to engage students in high levels of interaction	Classroom space is organized into learning stations for • Whole-class, paired, and small-group learning. • Students to consistently view graphic organizers, key vocabulary, and essential questions as they learn.	• Students sit in an area devoted to whole-class meetings. Either they move their desks into pairs and small-group meetings for group work or, as in elementary schools, classrooms are organized for these varied types of groupings. Teacher may sit with groups, pairs, or the whole class. • Essential questions, graphic organizers, and key vocabulary are displayed in predictable areas in the classroom that are known to students.
Focus lesson: "I do it"	A mini-lesson is taught directly by the teacher. It includes • The teacher's thinking, understanding, and modeling of the skill to be learned. • Explicit acknowledgment of students' identified assets and strengths. • Connections with students' lives and experiences to support their successful completion of a strategy, skill, or task to be learned. • Use of graphic organizers, anchor charts, and guiding or essential questions used.	Students sit in pairs or small groups. Teacher uses information from the mini-lesson and explicit acknowledgment of assets and strengths, connections to students' lives, and students making choices (e.g., texts to read, activities that they will do to learn).

(Figure continues on next page)

Figure 3.3 | Gradual Release of Responsibility *(continued)*

Components	Description	Examples
Guided instruction: "We do it"	The teacher facilitates learning, meets with small groups of students, and supports, encourages, and addresses needs of individual students in using different skills, strategies, and procedures independently.	Students ask and answer questions, working alongside peers.
Collaborative learning: "You do it together"	Collaborative learning allows students to process and discuss information with peers while their teacher clarifies, supports, and moves among groups.	Students work in small groups, collaborate, and share outcomes.
Independent work: "You do it alone"	Independent work allows students to synthesize what they have learned and solidify understanding.	Students work by themselves and are in control of outcomes.

Take a Closer Look: Illustrating the Gradual Release of Responsibility

The following lesson, intended for a grade span of 3rd to 5th grade students, demonstrates how another teacher, Jennifer Leigh, uses routines and practices that support students living with trauma, violence, and chronic stress in having routines that they can rely on. It is an activity about students' family heritage. Along with developing students' oral communication and literacy skills, the social-emotional purpose of the lesson is to help students get to know each other, develop a sense of belonging and of being valued, and build caring and empathetic relationships by sharing a family treasure that is important to them. It demonstrates how lessons can be adapted to ensure they are inclusive for our diverse student populations. For example, students are asked to bring in a family treasure. When Jennifer initially taught this unit, she found that some of her students had lost all of their family's mementos when they left their apartment and moved first to their family's car and then to a series of homeless shelters. In addition to asking students to bring in a family treasure, she now suggests that students can interview a family member, draw a picture of a treasure they once had, or tell a story about a family treasure.

Here is what this approach and lesson topic look like in action.

Step 1: Focus Lesson. Jennifer Leigh excitedly shares with her students that the lesson is intended to help them get to know each other by sharing their family's heritage. She tells students that they will be bringing in and sharing a family treasure, sharing an interview they had with a family member, drawing a picture of a treasure that they had to leave behind, or telling a family story. She explains that the treasure can be an artifact, photographs, drawings, or other mementos or recollections from their ancestors or others that their family values. Jennifer then conducts a mini-lesson in which she shares a family treasure that she possesses, an engraved locket that her great-grandmother brought with her to the United States from France in 1939 at the beginning of World War II. She explains why the locket is important to her family and what it means to her.

She then shows students a graphic organizer of how she organized her sharing activity, a reporting skill she wants them to learn that involves an oral and a written component. Jennifer then discusses how students will talk about their treasure and uses the graphic organizer to show them the process of using the same steps that she has modeled in the mini-lesson.

She asks students to talk with a partner about possible family treasures that they might share. Students begin to brainstorm various ideas of their own, choosing with the graphic organizer in hand.

Step 2: Guided Practice. Students brainstorm questions that they want to ask about the family treasure, including the various ways in which they can complete the task using the graphic organizer. Jennifer then asks guiding questions and leads students through the task (Fisher, 2015). Students share the steps that they will take to complete the task. During this step, she spends extra time with students who may be living with trauma, violence, and chronic stress to support them in identifying a family treasure, ways that they may discuss it, and elicit language that they can use to describe their family treasure. She knows that one of her students experienced a natural disaster. She asks questions such as, "Why is this (artifact, photograph, memento) important to your family? Why do you call this a treasure? Who does this (artifact, photograph, memento) come from? How are they related to you?" She uses the opportunity to learn from them and to identify values and qualities she can reflect back to them. This example demonstrates how Jennifer is encouraging student voice by allowing them to choose an artifact and fostering engagement by making learning relevant for them.

Step 3: Collaborative Learning. Jennifer's students show their artifact, photo, drawing of the artifact, or memento and share their treasure with a small group. Peers ask questions about each other's treasures using the skills and strategies that they were taught during Steps 1 and 2. This is an opportunity for students to acknowledge positive values and qualities in each other with proper modeling from the teacher.

Step 4: Independent Work. Students work independently in class to prepare their oral presentations. There are assigned spaces in the classroom suitable for independent work for those students who prefer to work in a space free of distraction. Jennifer suggests that they also practice their presentation with a family member or friend. They practice by independently using the sentence frames that they co-developed during Step 3. For example,

This (artifact, photograph, memento) is important to my family because . . .

This (artifact, photograph, memento) is called a . . .

It comes from my . . . (relative or ancestor) . . . (name).

It is used to . . .

Time for Reflection

Design a lesson that includes the four steps in the gradual release of responsibility approach and describe the routines and practices that you would use.

The following strategies are helpful for lesson planning and delivery. As stated earlier, they can be used with all students but are particularly beneficial for students who live with trauma, violence, and chronic stress.

- Prepare a study guide for students at their learning level to help organize information and reduce uncertainty. The study guide will help students who are experiencing adversity and others organize material and will provide a sense of order and consistency.
- Provide information about the steps needed to engage in a task, and include examples.
- Provide students with a description of an assignment or task and a clear set of criteria.
- Chunk content-area learning into small sections, providing students with ample breaks. Examples of this include short video clips or the completion of a few math problems.
- Scaffold information so that students can learn new content. Scaffolds include think-alouds, tapping into prior knowledge, preteaching vocabulary, and using visual aids.
- Infuse lessons with experience-based learning. Examples include visits to businesses, doctor's and dentist's offices, hospitals, libraries, the fire station, the police station, a pet store, government offices, a local city, or a farm.

Chapter 4 discusses the importance of student-to-student relationships and learning. Pair and small-group learning have been proven to be a powerful method of supporting students who are living with trauma, violence, and chronic stress and helping them feel a sense of belonging and feel safe, valued, and competent. Chapter 4 focuses on this important method.

Scaffolding Student-to-Student Relationships

We can improve our relationships with others by leaps and bounds if we become encouragers instead of critics.

—Joyce Meyer

Throughout this book, we have stressed the importance of positive, asset-based interactions in educating students living with trauma, violence, and chronic stress. In this chapter, we turn our focus to student-to-student interactions, particularly as applied to diverse classroom settings where some students are living with trauma, violence, and chronic stress. We look at three elements that are critical for collaborative learning:

1. Creating, implementing, and reflecting on pair and small-group learning experiences.

2. Apprenticing students in the social and emotional communicative skills needed in collaborative school settings.

3. Sparking student interest in learning and using consistent, predictable cooperative learning routines and rituals.

Creating, Implementing, and Reflecting on Pair and Small-Group Learning Experiences

An abundance of educational research has shown that learning is enhanced when it is a highly active, interactive process and interdependent endeavor and that learning cooperatively enhances the promotion of social skills as well as student empowerment (Cohen & Lotan, 2014; Johnson & Johnson, 2009; Johnson, Johnson, & Holubec, 2008; Sharan, 1990). In this chapter, we show that the same holds true for students living with trauma, violence, and chronic stress, particularly when we teach to our students' strengths. Various educational scholars have used a range of definitions and terms to describe cooperative learning. We use Sharan's (1990) definition, as it is specific but also comprehensive. Sharan defines cooperative learning—what many refer to as collaborative, small-group, pair, or group learning—as a community effort in which two to six participants are heterogeneously grouped to "work together to complete a group goal, share ideas, and help each other with answers to questions, share materials, and divide labor when appropriate" to complete a task (p. 2). A first and important task that will foster success is to examine the physical setup of our classrooms to ensure that they are conducive for collaboration.

Making Sure the Physical Setup Is Ready for Cooperation

When we plan to use pair or small-group cooperative learning, we have to consider the physical classroom space. Educational scholars Marshall and DeCapua (2014) warn that educators commonly neglect to pay attention to the classroom's physical setup, despite research showing that the placement of desks, tables, chairs, electronic equipment, and more has a significant effect on how well students interact with each other and teachers. They suggest creating a physical space that has moveable elements so that students can flexibly design the room in ways that work best for them and the collaborative activities they are engaged in. Chapter 3 highlighted the importance of creating a physical environment for students that fosters a sense of belonging and of feeling valued, competent, and safe.

Indeed, we want to create a positive classroom climate that becomes our students' home away from home. We want them to have a real say in the appearance of the room, what goes on the walls, and so forth. In addition to moving desks, tables, and chairs into arrangements that are conducive to pair and group work, it is important to consider how students will display their work so that the classroom is a communal space. This is especially true for students living with trauma, violence, and chronic stress, so that they are able to exercise some control over their learning environment. Marshall and DeCapua (2014) suggest that some of the classroom walls be devoted to student sharing of ideas, opinions, and concepts so that they have a real sense of ownership of their classroom space and academic learning.

 Time for Reflection

1. Using a blank piece of paper, map out a blueprint for a classroom space where pair and small-group work will occur. Show where students will display their work so that it is a shared space.

2. Explain how this space will be conducive to pair and small-group work.

Preparing Students for the Task and Process Elements of Cooperative Learning

Cooperative learning involves two elements: task and process. Let's say, for example, that a 5th grade social studies teacher tells five small groups composed of four students each, "Let's get into our groups and create a poster depicting the three branches of government in our democracy." We can picture a whole class of 20 students separated into small groups working on the poster creation *task* that they have been assigned. Like the examples in Chapter 3, which described a 2nd grade mathematics lesson on odd and even numbers and a 3rd–5th grade language arts lesson on a family treasure, we might expect the 5th grade teacher to use a gradual release of responsibility to engage students in the task. We would expect to see the teacher describing the thinking and understanding of the skills to be learned, modeling the ways students should engage in the poster-making project, and then having students work in groups to create it.

While we can picture these pair and small-group learning experiences occurring, we have to consider how we will attend, and help our students attend, to two elements that are present in *all* pair and small-group work at all grade levels: the assigned task and the process by which students will collaborate (Figure 4.1).

Figure 4.1 | Elements of Cooperative Learning

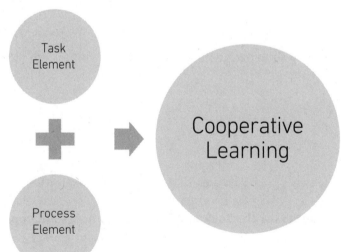

Understanding the Task Element of Pair and Group Work

The first element is the task that we assign to pairs, triads, or small groups. Here are some examples of a collaborative task assignment:

- Create a poster.
- Prepare a presentation.
- Write a play.
- Respond to a question.

Included in our thinking about this collaborative task element must be how to spark students' individual and collective engagement in it. If you recall, Chapter 3 discussed the importance of fostering student engagement through promoting students' voice. Individuals who live in traumatic situations are likely to experience a complete loss of control and sense of powerlessness. We pointed to the urgency of supporting students in regaining control by implementing practices that value and encourage students' participation in decisions that matter to them (Perry & Szalavitz, 2006).

Chapter 3 included a 2nd grade activity in which students found solutions to the challenges they were experiencing at recess using the mathematical concepts they were studying. It also included a unit of study that required upper elementary school students to create a presentation about a personal family treasure. Teachers used pair and group work in both. In this chapter, we present a high school chemistry teacher and the choices she makes to support students' empowerment and voice in studying the phenomena of a chemical reaction while engaging in collaborative learning.

Understanding the Process Component of Pair and Group Work

The second component of pair and group work is the process, which requires that students gather, work, and collaborate in a number of cooperative interactions. This includes sharing their beliefs or ideas about what they are learning, deliberating about these ideas collectively, and coming to agreement about them. The ways in which students communicate with each other is a critical factor. Let's look at an example of the process component in action.

Janetta Wallace is a high school chemistry teacher in a community near Cleveland, Ohio. Many of her lessons involve lab experiments that require students to work in pairs or small groups. She has just separated her class into the same small-group configuration as we showed in our earlier example of the 5th grade class. In addition, she directs students almost identically to the 5th grade teacher by saying, "Please get into our lab groups, and discuss the steps we will take to conduct our experiment." As she walks among the groups, she hears this exchange:

> Jamal: Hey, we are supposed to be looking at these lab steps. What's your problem?
> James: Huh?
> Jamal: Are you listening to me?
> James: [No response]
> Alyssa: Wow, Jamal, you are pretty pushy today. Pushy, pushy, pushy!
> Jackie: James, I am here for you. Want me to share what Mrs. Wallace asked us to do?
> James: [No response]
> Jamal: [Expletive] you, James! You are ridiculous.
> James: Whatever.
> Jackie: Now, Jamal, come on. It's no big deal. Hey, we can do this! Let's go over what Mrs. Wallace said. I think I remember the steps. First, she asked us to do this . . .
> Jamal: [Expletive] you, too!

Here is what Janetta knows about two of the students, James and Jamal. Each has experienced significant trauma in his life, and she has met with their guidance counselor to seek his support in teaching them. She knows that James's twin brother was killed in a car accident, his father was recently laid off from work (as many in their community have been), and the family is struggling to cope with the loss of both their son and their sole source of income. Janetta also knows that Jamal's mother has been deployed multiple times to Afghanistan and then Iraq and that Jamal and his family live in constant fear that she will be killed.

What we sometimes see in students experiencing trauma, violence, and chronic stress are interactions with peers that reflect the difficulties they may have in forming trusting relationships with others, sharing their feelings, and attending to tasks, as well as experiencing helplessness and a lack of control of their lives (Blaustein, 2013). Collaborative learning has been proven to be a powerful method for creating a classroom environment that promotes a sense of belonging, safety, value, and competency—especially when peers bolster these behaviors. But adults need to create the right circumstances for these behaviors to be displayed and acknowledge and reflect them back to students when they occur.

Apprenticing Students in the Social and Emotional Communicative Skills Needed in Collaborative School Settings

Figure 1.1: Circles of Interactions (see p. 20) illustrates the communication that children have with others during their development. Children learn how to act and behave through repeated exposure to, observations of, and interactions with their home and family communities. When students reach school age, they should be engaged in the same types of learning actions in their classrooms. That is, we should guide them in how to act and behave through repeated exposure to, observations of, and interactions with their classroom community while we tap into their own inherent values and qualities. This is often critical for students living with trauma, violence, and chronic stress and others who may have not had the privilege of exposure and opportunity to fully develop the social and emotional communicative skills that are needed in school settings and elsewhere in their lives (Bernard & Newell, 2013; Blaustein, 2013; Hertel & Johnson, 2013; Wiebler, 2013). As such, we must support students in engaging in pair and group work.

Supporting Students in Using Asset-Based Pair and Group Work Communication

Educational scholar Rachel Lotan (2006) discusses the importance of taking time to identify, acknowledge, and value students' strengths and assets.

She suggests that we can do this by identifying and honoring the many types of intelligences or "smarts" that our students possess by acknowledging them when they are demonstrated. First, we must closely observe and interact with our students so that we can find their strengths. And we do that by relentlessly looking for evidence with which we can validate qualities of inner wealth (Grove & Glasser, 2007). These initial efforts represent a first move toward helping students experience the four essentials that we have presented throughout this book: that students feel safe, valued, competent, and a sense of belonging in our classrooms.

Earlier chapters presented various strategies for engaging in these types of relationship-building tasks and activities. Implementing these principles and practices does much more than demonstrate to our students that we care for and about them (which is critical in and of itself). It also demonstrates to them how to care about and for each other by repeatedly having them engage with each other and observe us consistently and continuously interacting positively with them and their peers. As such, we routinely help students develop the social and emotional language that is needed to flourish in school settings and elsewhere (Bernard & Newell, 2013; Grove & Glasser, 2007; Hertel & Johnson, 2013).

Childhood trauma and chronic stress affect a large portion of the student population, regardless of where we work. And the influence of these phenomena can be far-reaching. The loss of a twin sibling, as we described for James, and living in constant fear that a family member will be killed while deployed abroad, as we described for Jamal, affect these students as well as their families. Clinical psychologist and director of the Trauma Training and Education Division at the Trauma Center at Justice Resource Institute, in Brookline, Massachusetts, Margaret Blaustein (2013) explains that many of the responses students express in school may be the result of repeated exposure to the stress they experience in their lives. As educators, we genuinely need to find ways to better ensure our students' safety, sense of belonging, and sense of being valued and seen as competent. However, we often do not consider the support that we need and the amount of time and repeated practice that our students require for them to successfully develop the social, emotional, and communicative skills needed to engage with each other effectively in collaborative learning settings.

While we might feel that some experiences are too challenging to overcome, Blaustein (2013) highlights some of the critical scaffolds that we can and must use to create a safe, successful learning environment for all of our students. Thus far in this book, we have discussed showing students that we care for and about them by taking time to identify their strengths and assets and drawing from these in our work with them. The same ideology applies as we prepare students to work with each other. We must use an approach that is directly aimed at creating a learning environment that is energizing, affirming, and focused on effort and assets. Just as we want students to learn with and from each other, we need to do the same to build an asset-based tool kit that we can readily use in our classrooms.

Learning About Students Living with Trauma, Violence, and Chronic Stress

First, it is tremendously helpful for us to learn as much information as possible about students living with trauma, violence, and chronic stress from the mental and behavioral specialists with whom we work (Chapter 6 discusses this in detail). If we look at Janetta Wallace, from earlier in the chapter, we see that she met with her school's guidance counselor to learn about James and Jamal. As a general practice, meetings with counselors, social workers, nurses, and school psychologists are quite helpful in building instructional programming for our students. They bolster our ideas and practices for creating an environment that focuses on students' social and emotional communicative language development.

According to applied behavioral analyst Ladona Wiebler (2013), students' abilities to "get along with each other is a growth process that must be nurtured if they are to be successful as adults" (p. 39). She speaks to the reality that students develop social and emotional communication at different rates. It is akin to learning a new language; students living with trauma, violence, and chronic stress and others are at differing stages of social-emotional communication development (e.g., emerging, developing, integrating, enacting).

Understanding Social-Emotional Language Learning as a Development Process

A factor to consider when applying the method of cooperative learning, therefore, is that not all students work and communicate alike. One means to support the method more successfully is enhancing the level of trust we create with all of our students and that students create with each other. We must develop trust because students have to be secure in knowing that we will provide them with "consistency, predictability, structure, and the opportunity to develop caring relationships" (Wiebler, 2013, p. 40). Previous chapters presented strategies for ensuring that this occurs between students and ourselves. When we apply these to the planning and designing of pair and small-group tasks, the following supports are crucial:

- Classrooms must be ideal places for students to acquire the social and emotional communicative skills that they need to work cooperatively.
- All students need this type of instruction so that everyone feels safe, valued, a sense of belonging, and competent. While this is especially critical for students experiencing trauma, violence, and chronic stress, it is important for all students.

Building Students' Social and Emotional Language Skills

We might think that teaching primarily involves the content or subject matter that we are tasked with (e.g., mathematics, English language arts, social studies, biology), but our instruction also involves helping students develop and use the following:

- Listening skills.
- Empathy.
- Social and emotional language that is needed to express their feelings to their peers and others.
- Attention to their own and their peers' values, assets, and strengths.
- Mediating their own emotions.
- Resolution of conflict in a productive way.

We have to design pair and group work with plans that explicitly and intentionally support students in the development of these skills in a productive, positive way. We also look for opportunities within these groups to recognize the many ways in which students, overtly or covertly, demonstrate their personal assets.

Assigning Pairs, Groups, and Roles in Cooperative Learning Using Meaningful Tasks

Our goal should always be to provide students with a positive and successful experience. Initially, it is much safer and more predictable to assign students to work in pairs as opposed to small groups, especially as they begin to use the model of cooperative learning. While we may later move students into small groups, we have to consider that this method must be carefully, sensitively, and explicitly planned, designed, and implemented for it to work. Hence, pair work is a more ideal setting for this to initially occur.

Wiebler (2013) suggests that we do this by placing students living with trauma, violence, and chronic stress with partners who have already developed strong empathy and social skills. In addition, seminal cooperative learning theorists Johnson and Johnson (2009) and Johnson, Johnson, and Holubec (2008) discuss the importance of deliberately assigning students to specific pairs or small groups and giving them specific roles to play (e.g., project manager, project recorder).

 Time for Reflection

Revisit the exchange among the four students in Janetta Wallace's class.

1. You plan to separate the group of four into two groups of two. Which students (James, Jamal, Alyssa, Jackie) would you pair together and why?

2. What steps do you believe are important to take in order to prepare the pairs that you have selected to work together?

Once we have placed students in pairs, it is imperative that we model and teach them how to be effective listeners. A helpful means to do this at all grade levels is to explicitly assign pairs of students the role of listener and speaker. We can then assign listeners to engage in a particular listening act. It is also crucial to assign a task that is compelling and engaging so that students will be energized to complete it. As students engage in listening and speaking actions, it is also a time to intentionally look for students who show even the simplest way of listening and acknowledge it as a human virtue already in them.

Let's look at an example from Janetta Wallace's class, where groups of students will be tasked with doing a lab experiment on chemical reactions. Janetta knows that her school is located near railroad tracks. In fact, once a day, a train travels by the school. She knows that students have this background experience on which to draw. So on the first day of the unit of study on chemical reactions, she takes her students on a short walking trip to see the railroad tracks. She tells them that they will be studying how engineers hold the tracks together. They then return to her classroom. On the interactive whiteboard, Janetta projects a photo of an aerial view of a railroad track that extends for miles and miles over mountains and rivers and so forth. She shares with her students that engineers have come up with ways to join the railway tracks together and allow trains to run smoothly without having to carry or haul in large loads of metal to weld the pieces together. She tells them that they will be engaging in a lab that will cause a chemical reaction and that their lab experience will be quite similar to the one that engineers use. Next to the photograph, she has posted the following directions:

> Speaker: How do you think engineers are able to join these tracks together for miles and miles without having to haul in tons of metal to weld the tracks together? Suggest at least one idea as a possible response.
>
> Listener: Listen carefully to your partner's idea, and discuss why you believe it might be a possible way for joining the tracks together. If your partner provides more than one response, select the one that makes the most sense to you, and tell her the reasons it makes the most sense.

Janetta tells the class that, in pairs, one person will be the speaker and the other the listener. She then separates her class into assigned pairs and asks them to select their roles. Pointing to the whiteboard, she reads the directions aloud. She tells students that all of their ideas are important and there is no such thing as a bad idea. Before engaging them in the task, she models what she wants students to do by enacting the role of listener and speaker aloud for them. She then asks students to complete the task just as she has.

Janetta places Jackie and James together, and James asks Jackie to be the speaker. When Jackie is finished explaining her ideas (she has more than one!), James hesitantly volunteers the one that makes the most sense to him.

Figure 4.2 displays the sequence of steps taken to engage students in pair learning. These include using the principles and strategies for building relationships with our students; seeking support from counseling staff about students living with trauma, violence, and chronic stress; assigning students to specific partners we believe have the best chance to be successful; assigning a compelling task that requires the enactment of listener and speaker roles; modeling the roles aloud; engaging students in the role; and acknowledging students' efforts throughout.

Apprenticing Students into Pair and Small-Group Experiences

Every segment of the cycle shown in Figure 4.2 is important. They provide critical space for

- Teachers to actively listen for students' use of positive social and emotional language.

Figure 4.2 | Cycles of Engaging Students in Pair Work

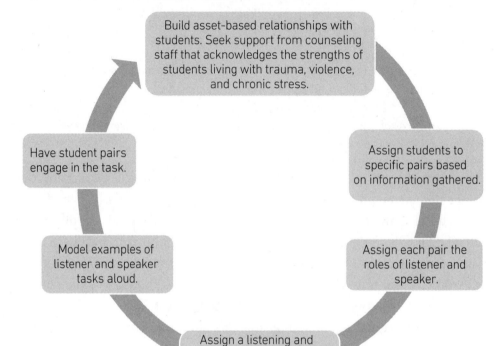

Build asset-based relationships with students. Seek support from counseling staff that acknowledges the strengths of students living with trauma, violence, and chronic stress.

Have student pairs engage in the task.

Assign students to specific pairs based on information gathered.

Model examples of listener and speaker tasks aloud.

Assign each pair the roles of listener and speaker.

Assign a listening and speaking task that is compelling by engaging students' voices and choices.

- Students to observe teachers' use of positive social and emotional language.
- Students to have multiple opportunities to practice using this language.

Indeed, these are incredibly important teachable moments that should not be skipped. They provide students with repeated exposure to the type of asset-based social and emotional language that people need to acquire for everyday communication with peers and others.

Figure 4.3 includes some examples of the type of language that we might use to acknowledge students' pair work efforts while they are engaging in it and afterward as a whole-class activity. The list has been drawn from Grove

Figure 4.3 | Asset-Based Language to Describe Students' Efforts

That is excellent use of logic.	You are being wise. That is a great quality that is coming across in your responses.	That was a very insightful thought you just shared.	That was a solid educated guess. That is an important skill.
I appreciate your willingness to collaborate.	You seem to be getting the picture!	That was a great deduction you just made to figure out a possible answer. Well done!	You are showing great curiosity, which is a great way to learn.
The way you put these two ideas together shows how you are using great analytic skills in your problem solving.	I can see how much you are enjoying sharing and defending your unique ideas.	I really like how you are showing respect to your partner by listening carefully to what he is saying.	You are using your great mind to figure out an answer. Well done!

Source: Adapted from Grove and Glasser (2007, pp. 85–86). See the original for an expanded list of strengths-based language to encourage students' social and emotional language development.

and Glasser (2007), who suggest that we be specific in our positive language while reflecting back the values and attributes students have (who they are) and showing students that we have confidence in them.

 Time for Reflection

1. Create four or five additional statements that reflect values and qualities students have and are intended to support students' growing sense of confidence.

2. Describe two or three ways that you might encourage students to use this language with peers in pair and small-group settings.

Once students have experienced sufficient opportunities to engage in partner work successfully, we can move into small-group learning. Figure 4.4 shows the sequence of steps that should occur when launching students in small-group learning activities. First, we should engage students in the

Figure 4.4 | Cycle of Engaging Students in Small-Group Work

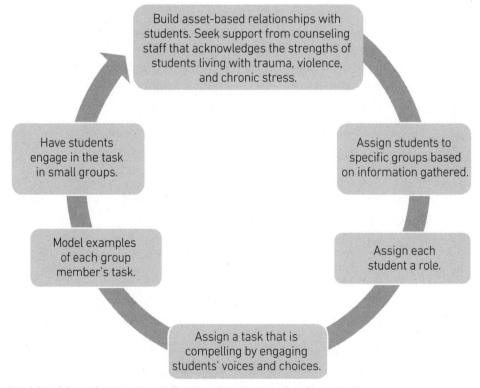

Note: Acknowledge student strengths and efforts throughout the stages of small-group work.

relationship-building activities described in Chapters 1–3. We should seek support from counseling staff about our specific students living with trauma, violence, and chronic stress. We should then assign students to groups that have the best chance of being successful. This includes partnering students who have developed more advanced social-emotional communication skills with students who are at earlier stages of this development. We should then assign roles and tasks that are compelling and best ensure students' interest in enacting the roles. An effective way to do this is by engaging students' voices and choices in the process. We should also model each role assignment to provide students with much-needed time to see it in action before they engage in it. We should then engage students in the cooperative learning task. As students engage in each part of the process of working in small groups, as well as at the conclusion of the assigned task as a whole class, we should acknowledge their efforts. Acknowledgment of efforts is an ongoing process, not something to provide solely at the end. It must be embedded throughout our interactions with students and their interactions with each other.

As in our pair work sequence, every segment of small-group work is powerfully important. As in our example of the pair sequence, engaging students in group work provides time for the following:

- Teachers to actively listen for students' use of positive social and emotional language.
- Students to observe teachers' use of positive social and emotional language.
- Students to have multiple opportunities to practice using this language.

According to Hertel and Johnson (2013), our goals should always be to continuously equip and empower students living with adversity with explicit instruction in the social and emotional communication skills that are needed for collaboration and to demonstrate to them that we value them unconditionally. Hertel and Johnson also share the importance of coaching students as they apprentice into using the type of communication that we are seeking in collaborative settings. Also, providing students with positive and detail-oriented feedback, such as the suggestions furnished in Figure 4.3, is essential to do. It is equally important to provide students with the language that is needed when things do not go well, acknowledge their ability and intention to be receptive to it, and use this language to show our confidence in them.

Supporting Positive Interactions by Teaching to Strengths

While we may have different approaches and strategies to stop the negative behaviors that can occur when we put students into pairs or small groups (e.g., the student who won't participate; the student who takes over a group, shuts down, fools around, or tries to get the group off task), whatever we do has to be a genuine effort to maintain students' feelings of being safe, belonging, being valued, and being competent. This is particularly true for students living with trauma, violence, and chronic stress. Students' feeling of competence is highly related to our doing whatever we can do to safeguard their confidence, their interest in learning, and their desire to do well.

As mentioned earlier, pairs may be the best means to enact the model initially, as they are small enough to best ensure that students are able to listen carefully to their peers and respond in kind. For example, in the exchange that occurred among the four students in Janetta's class, one challenged two others. We have found that this type of heated exchange is far less likely to occur in an assigned pair or group setting and when we take time to design and implement activities that are energizing and positively focused.

In the exchange that occurred among the four students, for example, one of them swore. Some of our schools have consequences for this type of negative verbal behavior, including sending a student to the school office or suspension from school for a prescribed period of time. We are not alone in our belief that this remedy may be counterproductive. Grove and Glasser (2007) have found the most effective response to be what they refer to as a "quick reset": a short, quick form of a timeout that can enable a quick return or reconnect to the task at hand. Here is an example of the reset in play.

Janetta Wallace is circulating throughout the room while James, Jamal, Alyssa, and Jackie are working, and she hears Jamal swear. She taps Jamal on the shoulder and whispers in his ear, "Jamal, do you need a short reset? We can ask the group to wait a minute for you." Grove and Glasser (2007) call this a "clean time out." It's one in which we don't give a lecture or say something that is negative, like "Stop that!" Rather, it gives students the opportunity to shift attention back to the task at hand without losing face with or being humiliated in front of their peers. And, most importantly, it does not take the student away from the learning environment.

You may believe that some students will take advantage of the situation and use it to avoid engaging with their peers. We believe that when we are clear in our intentions, when we show our patience and commitment to our students, and when we consistently and routinely show them that we are patient and that we care, they are much more likely to form trusting relationships with us. In addition, when we train our students to be patient with each other in the same manner that we model, they are much more likely to do the same once a trusting and caring relationship has been built. This can be better accomplished when we make it a habit to circulate through our classrooms while students are engaging in paired and group work so that we can listen, see, and support students' interactions as they are occurring.

Sparking Student Interest in Learning and Using Consistent, Predictable Cooperative Learning Routines and Rituals

Another important reason to observe and interact with students is to connect what is to be learned with what is *meaningful and compelling* for them. Of all the choices available to Janetta in terms of science experiments, she wanted to choose one that she thought would be the most fun and exciting for her students. She also wanted to pique their curiosity. She posed several ideas to explore chemical reactions. One was around how it was possible to lay thousands of miles of railroad tracks, which students identified as of interest.

Throughout the lesson on chemical reactions, this level of interest and adventure contributed to her students' willingness to engage in the types of group behaviors that she knew were needed.

Simultaneously, it is imperative that we use consistent and predictable learning routines and rituals. Chapters 2 and 3 provided a range of strategies for using consistent, predictable routines and practices. The same ideology must be used when engaging students in collaborative work.

According to Bernard and Newell (2013), our instruction in helping students develop the social and emotional communication skills that they need must include the following:

- Precise expressions and understandings of verbal and nonverbal cues.
- Appropriate play skills for younger children such as sportsmanship and inviting, joining, and ending play [activities].
- Rewarding (energizing) positive interactions.
- Modeling proper etiquette, problem solving peer disputes, and processing through negative interactions. (p. 213)

For example, Janetta helped James, Jamal, Alyssa, and Jackie solve a dispute that they were having about the various roles (e.g., project manager, materials manager, lab recording manager, safety and time manager) that were required to conduct the lab experiment. James and Alyssa both wanted the role of project manager. Janetta calmly did what she routinely does during these disputes. She listened carefully to the various perspectives and repeated what each student had said using positively oriented language. For example, when Alyssa said she should be the project manager because "I know more than anyone in the group," Janetta responded accordingly, "Alyssa would like to be project manager because she believes that she has worked very hard to learn the content." She coached the group to achieve a positive resolution. They decided collectively that James would be this lab experiment's project manager and that Alyssa would be the project manager in an experiment the following week. In addition, Janetta sought ways to create many consistent opportunities for the peers to engage in positive interactions.

Many school districts across the country, including urban districts such as Anchorage, Austin, Cleveland, Atlanta, Chicago, and El Paso, are engaged in using positive, explicit social-emotional communication instruction as part of their "practice of promoting integrated academic, social and emotional learning for all children in preschool through high school" (Collaborative for Academic, Social, and Emotional Learning, 2016). A common thread among these school districts and others is a focus on the social-emotional language that is needed for students to express their feelings to peers and others, attend to their own and their peers' needs and desires, mediate their emotions, and resolve conflict in a productive way. Supporting students to identify and name their feelings and develop empathy for others is an important feature to the teaching of social and emotional language.

In addition, it is important that we work as closely as possible with students' families using the strengths-based approach that is included throughout this book. In the next chapter, we look closely at understanding and identifying families' strengths and discuss practices and strategies for working more successfully and effectively with diverse students and families experiencing trauma, violence, and chronic stress.

Fostering Family/Guardian Engagement

*The ways schools care about children is reflected in the
way schools care about the children's families.*

—Joyce L. Epstein,
School, Family, and Community Partnerships

While we know that family-school partnerships are critical for our students'
success, and the research on this is clear, not many school personnel have had
training to work with families. We often learn how to do this as we are doing
it, while we are "on the job" (Henderson, Mapp, Johnson, & Davies, 2007).
What can make this seem all the more daunting a task is the reality that our
students' families are all too often quite different from our own. For example,
earlier in the book, we described the various types of family constellations that
exist in contemporary society. This includes students who are being reared by
two parents, a single parent, a blended family, grandparents, unrelated people who live cooperatively, foster parents, and with significant support from
extrafamilial individuals (Zacarian & Silverstone, 2015). For many of us, there
is also the challenge of creating partnerships with families who are culturally,
economically, and linguistically distinct from our own. In addition, a family's
vision of involvement in their child's school may be different from our own

and depend on such sweeping variables as their circumstances, past experiences, preferences, comfort, and more.

As such, while we may be familiar and more comfortable working with a particular type of family constellation or family background, we must become more and more comfortable, conscious, and competent in working with families whose configurations and backgrounds are different—sometimes vastly different—from our own. In addition, we often refer to the diversity among our student populations in the same way that our schools and districts report this information to state and national departments of education: as racial groups, English learners, students with disabilities, and students receiving free or reduced-price lunch. While this is important information to know, it is essential that we have a depth of understanding about these factors so we can work most successfully with our students and families, particularly those who experience significant adversity. We must also avoid the pitfalls of having preconceptions, or what social justice scholar Paul Gorski (2008) calls myths, about marginalized families. We have to be aware of the preconceptions, stereotypes, and myths that each of us can have about the families we work with. Some of these myths include such stereotypes as the beliefs that all poor families share the same way of being and acting, are "unmotivated and have weak work ethics," are uninvolved in their children's school because they do not value education, are linguistically deficient, and "tend to abuse drugs and alcohol" (Gorski, 2008). Stereotypes such as these can and do greatly affect our capacity to work successfully with families.

Think of how some of us might view students living with trauma, violence, and chronic stress. Some of us feel so sympathetic toward them that we might miss the strengths that the family possesses, including their capacity to cope with such circumstances. An example of this is Alicia Herrick, an urban middle school social studies teacher who worked with one of us. Every time Alicia found out she had a student who had experienced a significant stressor (e.g., a family member being incarcerated; anticipation of the death of a family member; experience with civil strife, war, or natural disasters in their home country; being undocumented), she would gather all of her own children's old clothing and bring it to the families of the students she believed were the most in need. She couldn't understand why some of the families refused to accept her gift. She also could not see these families as having much in the way of strengths. Rather, she made assumptions about them. Her stance was that they were too stressed to care for their children. These beliefs clouded her capacity to see what she didn't know, despite her wanting to do the best that she could on behalf of her students.

This chapter follows Alicia as she moves from using a deficit-based approach to a strengths-based approach to foster family/guardian engagement. It discusses the importance of challenging the preconceived beliefs, even subconscious ones, that we possess so that we may demonstrate to families our genuine capacity to create meaningful and sustained partnerships with them on behalf of their children's academic success and the future. This discussion draws from the field of social work, as it has a long history of research-proven practices for working with children and families experiencing trauma, violence, and chronic stress. The chapter provides specific steps that we can take to help families living with trauma, violence, and chronic stress see their own strengths and empower them to use these to create their own portfolio or personal account of strengths and assets. It also provides tools and strategies for building trusting, caring, and engaging partnerships with families. Although the main focus is families and students living in powerfully challenging situations, these tools and strategies are also useful for creating strong, positive, and engaging relationships with all students' families.

Educational scholars Henderson and colleagues (2007) use the term *partnerships* to define the special qualities of this reciprocal school-family involvement. The term is also used by Zacarian and Silverstone (2015) to describe the positive possibilities that can and do occur when students, educators, parents, and community members work together. This chapter shows how to employ a partnership ideology with families. It draws from the growing body of research and evidence about the importance of using a strengths-based approach to build partnerships—particularly with families experiencing the challenges of trauma, violence, and chronic stress.

We begin by looking closely at an exchange between Alicia and the school's social worker. Alicia shares that she has attempted to meet with several of her students' families. She also expresses her frustration that, once again, only a very small percentage of her students' families have come to the routine parent-teacher conferences that she has scheduled: "I really want to get to know my students' families. But many have not shown up for my scheduled parent-teacher conferences, and I have heard they don't show up for school events or meetings either." She then asks the social worker, "What can I do?"

Perhaps you have been involved in this type of exchange—the one in which you wholeheartedly want to figure out the best means to solve a problem. In this exchange, Alicia asks the school's social worker for help in creating more effective ways to address the problem of family participation. She seeks support from someone who represents a field that has done a lot of research and shown sound evidence for an approach that we should all use. Indeed, we can learn a great deal from the social work field about how to work with families experiencing trauma, violence, and chronic stress.

Moving from What We Don't Know

Prior to the 1980s, general social work practices called for approaches that were based on identifying the pathology of an individual, family, or community system (Pulla, 2012; Saleebey, 1996). Whether it was an identified deficit, disorder, abnormality, or problem, the accepted approach was to treat what was wrong. The lack of positive and sustained outcomes moved the field from using a deficit-based approach to one that called for acknowledging difficulties *and* creating opportunities for families and social workers to work together to identify and draw from families' strengths. As such, during the past several decades, the social work field has largely shifted from using a deficit-based approach to using an asset-based one to treat families in distress and secure lasting solutions (Early, 2001). The outcomes of this transformation show its promise. Let's return to Alicia to see how we may apply some of the key principles for using what social work scholars Saint-Jacques, Turcotte, and Pouliot (2009) aptly describe as a *strengths perspective*.

A strengths perspective comes from securing knowledge about families' strengths to develop strong, lasting, and mutually fulfilling partnerships with them. Because so many of us have not had any formal education in working with families, let alone partnering with them, we have to consider (as the field of social work has) how to learn as much as we can about how to work successfully with families experiencing trauma, violence, and chronic stress. Learning anything involves a process of acquiring the knowledge, skills, and practices associated with it, and this process involves four stages (Roland & Matheson, 2012).

First Stage

In the first stage of learning, we don't know that we don't know something. Consider Alicia Herrick, our focal teacher. She knows that some of her students are experiencing or have experienced adversity. She acts on preconceived beliefs about these students. As Gorski (2008, para. 8) describes, in doing so, she brings to her work "the most common and dangerous myths" about people and parents. Take, for example, her beliefs about students from undocumented families. She believes that most live in poverty. Yes, being poor is an observable fact, given that Alicia knows these students receive free lunch and may observe that they lack the same resources that she and some of her other students have. However, this information does not provide her with any additional knowledge about the lives of these families, let alone about the strengths that her students and their families possess and how to use these to partner with families in support of students' social and cognitive development. Acquiring that level of knowledge and practice requires her to move from the first, myth-driven stage to the much-needed second stage.

Second Stage

In the second stage of professional growth, we consciously know that we don't know something. It also requires that we challenge the myths that we have been using and unlearn the misperceptions that we carry. For instance, it could be easy for Alicia to accept a myth that low-income families do not value education. Nevertheless, she acknowledges that this belief is too simplistic and undermines the value of each family and their unlimited potential to enrich our schools and classrooms. Indeed, research has clearly disputed the notion that low-income parents, such as those from undocumented families, lack interest in their children's education (Epstein, 1986, 2001; Epstein et al., 2009). While their involvement in school may be less than that of non-poor families due to socioeconomic conditions such as having to work multiple jobs, working evening hours, having limited or no paid leave and transportation, and dealing with child care challenges (Gorski, 2008), they are just as committed to their children.

During this stage of development, Alicia acknowledges that she does not know what she needs to know about students and families. And she begins to question the actions she has taken because she sincerely wants to strengthen the ways in which she works with students and families. She is aware of the preconceived notions she has been operating under, as well as her lack of knowledge, and she wants to do something about it. Her positive professional growth efforts point to the importance of building from and capitalizing on students' and families' cultural ways of being and acting. In doing so, she acknowledges and values her students' families as powerful resources. She can do this by taking time to get to know them as individuals, build relationships with them, and connect her students' learning to the knowledge she gains. As such, she wants to learn how to be a more effective partner with families living with trauma, violence, and chronic stress. She begins to take the steps needed to obtain this much-needed education and awareness.

In a real sense, this second stage involves two important components for Alicia: first, acquiring the knowledge she needs about students and families and second, and equally important, using this knowledge in her professional practice with students and families. As such, Alicia realizes that the steps she had taken (gathering and donating her own children's clothes), though seemingly a good gesture, supported her use of a deficit-based approach as opposed to the positive one that is needed. She realizes she has always viewed families in distress as lacking the resources and ability to help their children. She now understands that she has operated from this deficit-based stance. She also acknowledges that she doesn't have the understanding and skills needed to work with students and families living in these circumstances. As a result, she is doing what she needs to do to acquire this knowledge.

Third Stage

In the third stage, we take into account the knowledge and practices we have learned and employ them. During this stage, Alicia learns the principles and practices involved in using a strengths-based approach with families living with trauma, violence, and chronic stress. She monitors her actions carefully to make sure she consciously uses this approach with families. She frequently confers with the school's social worker and others to check in about her actions. She consciously and conscientiously makes sure to acknowledge families' strengths and, through her own self-monitoring, engages in self-correction to avoid her old pattern of viewing families negatively. For example, recently, a few families from Syria moved into her community. In the past, Alicia would have thought these families had no resources of their own and she would have quickly gone to her children's closets to see what clothes she could donate to them. Now, based on the knowledge and skills she has acquired and is consciously using, she knows the importance of learning all that she can about the families and students before taking any actions that would be inconsistent with an asset-based perspective.

Fourth Stage

In this last stage, we develop an internalized state of knowing and doing so that our thoughts and actions are second nature. Alicia now regards every family as an equal partner with her. While acknowledging families' circumstances, she focuses on their competencies and seeks ways to identify and draw from their strengths on behalf of their children. She goes a step further and empowers them by reflecting back the family's assets so they can cultivate their own image of their inner wealth. She no longer has to self-monitor her own actions, as they have been internalized to such a level that it is second nature for her to act in a positive manner. In fact, she has moved a step beyond; she's begun to support colleagues to work through the same stages of professional growth as she has.

Alicia is eager to support her peers as they engage in more successful partnerships with the range of family constellations and backgrounds that exist within their middle school family community. Recently, for example, undocumented immigrants who live in a nearby shelter have enrolled in the school. Alicia wants to learn all that she can about their prior personal, social, cultural, family, world, and schooling experiences so she can personalize her interactions with them and highlight the many strengths that each brings. With colleagues, she collaboratively creates plans to get to know the students and families. They also create a personal narrative activity for all new students so the school staff may learn about their students' life experiences. In addition, she has made plans with colleagues to meet with professionals who work at the shelter. The goal is to get to know the students and families on a personal level. We will learn more about this later in the chapter.

 Time for Reflection

1. Identify and describe a myth or misconception that you had about a group of people and the steps you took to acknowledge it.

2. Identify and describe a personal learning experience. What stages of learning did you complete?

3. Describe the core reasons that positively drove you to complete the four-stage learning experience you described in your response to question #2.

 Time for Reflection

1. Identify and describe a professional learning experience you had in which you completed the four stages of learning that we described in this chapter on behalf of your students and their families. (Note: Participants who are new to the field of teaching may draw from prior work experiences in another field to complete this task.)

2. Describe the core reasons that drove you through this four-stage learning experience.

Using Partnership Meetings to Learn About Students and Families

A first step in committing to understanding our students and their families living with trauma, violence, and chronic stress is showing our interest in getting to know them. All too often, schools can be cold and impersonal places. Think of enrollment. What do families typically do? They travel to their children's school or a centralized registration institution to complete a standard set of forms such as medical, prior schooling, and emergency contact documents. After the first few weeks or months, families are invited to their children's school to passively learn about their schooling at an Open House or Curriculum Night (Zacarian, 2011; Zacarian & Haynes, 2012; Zacarian & Silverstone, 2015). These are generally followed or preceded with parent-teacher conferences in which a teacher tells parents or guardians how their children are doing in school as the parents or guardians sit fairly passively to receive this information. None of these routine events has been found to truly engender the type of partnerships that reflect a true reciprocal commitment to families (Lawrence-Lightfoot, 2003; Zacarian & Silverstone, 2015).

Just as we adjust our professional practice to the unique learning needs of our students, particularly those who live with adversity, we need to show the same type of conscious responsiveness with their families. Earlier chapters talked about the importance of providing students with an environment where they feel safe and experience a real sense of belonging, of being competent, and of being valued (Grove & Glasser, 2007; Glasser, 2011). We want to make sure that we embed these essentials in our interactions with students' families. It is easy to do so when we genuinely believe that all families bring with them rich resources and rich opportunities for interactions. For instance, it could be easy to overlook the enormous amount of emotional and physical energy required for parents to send their children to school every day. Couple that with families who are living with trauma, violence, and chronic stress, and it should not be difficult to see the commitment, determination, and perseverance most of these families exhibit in spite of adversity. It is our moral responsibility to affirm these qualities, let the families know how much we value them, and use these assets in our classrooms and in our interactions with them.

Partnership meetings are an essential means for reaching out and learning about our student and family populations. They are foundational for building connections and, in doing so, building meaningful collaborations with families. They also can provide us with helpful information from which to strengthen our instructional programming. Here are a few things we must consider when planning a partnership meeting:

- The partnership meeting's purpose.
- How to conduct the meeting and who will attend.
- The topics to be discussed.
- The process by which information is shared with others.

The Partnership Meeting's Purpose

The purpose of the meeting is twofold. First, it is to build a connection and trust with families and students living with trauma, violence, and chronic stress. The process is intended to show families and students in a real way that we want to get to know them because we care about them. Second, it is to learn about the personal, social, world, cultural, and educational strengths, perspectives, and experiences of students and families. In doing so, we prepare ourselves to meet with families and students by being open-minded, not carrying prejudgments, and being totally receptive to everything we hear and see (Gonzáles, Moll, & Amanti, 2005). Our purpose in doing this is to build a classroom community and learning environment that draw from the background experiences of students and families.

How to Conduct the Meeting and Who Will Attend

All initial partnership meetings should be conducted face-to-face, if possible. Subsequent meetings might be conducted by phone or video chat to accommodate the family or student. Knowing that our schools may be filled with new students and families, and recognizing the challenges related to identifying which students and families need more of our attention, it is important to maintain open communication with the school's social worker, psychologist, nurse, and others who support students' psychological and overall well-being. Without question, whenever we have a concern about a student, for either psychosocial or academic reasons, we should engage in this process. In addition, building relationships with any family requires building trust between professionals and families. As such, whenever possible, staff should be trained to conduct these meetings for the sole purpose of building trusting relationships with families. It is also crucial to provide families with information, in advance, about the purpose of any meeting so that they can be prepared and not feel awkward. This is particularly true for families living with trauma, violence, and chronic stress, as it provides a helpful road map for understanding what will unfold during the meeting.

The traditional parent-teacher conference may be an ideal time for accomplishing this goal if we can redefine it as a time for getting to know families. Again, the goal of partnership meetings is to create a personal, connecting, and collaborative environment so that families know we truly care about them and their children. As such, teachers, counselors, and other school professionals/specialists should be trained to participate in these meetings. Also, the meetings should be conducted as early in an academic school year as possible and, of course, whenever new students arrive during the school year. They should also be conducted in welcoming spaces. For some families, the school may be a welcoming environment. For others, the home environment or a public space such as the local library may be an ideal location. When conducting partnership meetings in the family's home or a public space, some educators pair up with other school staff to impart the message that people from the school community care about and are interested in connecting with them.

When students and families are invited to a partnership meeting, we should give them information about its twofold purpose, as well as the start and end time for it. Figure 5.1 provides a sample invitation.

Figure 5.1 | Sample Invitation to a Family Partnership Meeting

Dear [Name],

I am greatly looking forward to working with you, your child, and our class community. I would welcome a meeting with you, your child, and any other family member you would like to include so that we may get to know one another. Together we want to create the most promising classroom community and learning environment for your child. I suggest the following date, time, and place for our meeting:

Date: Time: Place:

Please let me know if the date, time, or place will not work for you, and kindly suggest other options below:

Date: Time: Place:

I will follow up with a phone call soon.
Thank you very much, and I'm looking forward to meet you soon!

Sincerely,

[Teacher's Name]

The Topics to Be Discussed

Where a typical parent/guardian survey asks families to complete a fixed set of questions, the type of partnership meeting advocated here is personal, open-minded, less structured, and flexible. Ideally, we should exercise active listening (the same kind we ask from our students in the classroom) and pose questions that will provide us with a clear picture of the family's strengths and values as we build partnerships with them. Zacarian and Silverstone (2015) highlight the importance of conveying the following messages to families when we meet with them:

- We believe it's important to get to know each other.
- We value your participation.

- Our classroom is a community, and there's a place for you in it as we work together on behalf of your son or daughter.
- We are comfortable with your questions and welcome your engagement.

We understand that some families will be more talkative than others and that some may not be familiar with our schools. When facilitated by caring and empathetic professionals, a school tour can be an excellent time to begin building partnerships. To do this, we have to think carefully about our conversations with families. Whether during a tour or in a meeting with a family, our goal must be to convey our genuine interest in partnering with them. Although not intended to be an exhaustive list, the set of suggested topics and questions presented in Figure 5.2 has two purposes: to help us build partnerships by learning about the social, cultural, world, and educational experiences of our students and families and to help us identify some of the families' values and assets *and* reflect these back to them. As such, our goal is to support families in creating or enhancing their own inner wealth image, similar to what we proposed with students in Chapter 2.

It is also critical to set a welcoming and supportive tone when inviting families to any meeting. Newly enrolled students and families should be contacted for the purpose of building partnerships and drawing from the knowledge that is gained to plan and implement an instructional program based on students' and families' strengths. Figure 5.2 provides suggested topics, each of which is accompanied by an opening discussion question. These are intended to create as positive a partnership experience as possible. As with any meeting with families, we encourage and recommend the active participation of the upper elementary, middle, and high school students themselves. As such, the suggested questions should be modified for this purpose.

The Process by Which Information Is Shared with Others

As discussed earlier, the information gathered from these interactions should help us create trusting and caring relationships with families and

Figure 5.2 | Suggested Topics and Questions for Partnership Meetings

Topics	Suggested Questions
1. Find out about qualities and values that make the student unique to his or her family.	What makes [name of child] special (things that set him or her apart from others, qualities he or she has, things he or she values)?
2. Find out about what makes the relationship special between the parent and the student.	What are some things you enjoy about [name of child]?
3. Find out what qualities and values the parent appreciates from the student.	What particular talents and skills would you like me to know about [name of child]?
4. Find out about the family's values and how they share their life together.	What are things you enjoy doing as a family?
5. Find out about the family's likes and strengths to show that they are valued and they belong to the school community.	We want to be a welcoming place for you and your children. What would make the experience of coming to our school more enjoyable?
6. Set the stage for partnership and collaboration while valuing the family's input.	We see parents as our partners. Is there any particular way you would like to help me make your child's school experience a great one?
7. Set the stage for partnership and collaboration while leveraging the family's assets.	What special talents or interests would you consider sharing with the students in [name of child's] class or with students' families?
8. Find out about family's values and dreams for the student, and acknowledge them as family assets.	What are your hopes and dreams for [name of child's] education?
9. Set the stage for honesty, trust, partnership, and collaboration, along with a clear message of inclusiveness and belonging.	What questions do you wish I had asked and would like to be sure are included?

become partners with them in their children's education. The information that we gather will help us develop interventions and strategies that will capitalize on the best of our students' family life. Also, as emphasized earlier, it is essential that we communicate to families, in words and actions, that we value them, we believe they are competent individuals whom we can count on, and they have a place in our classrooms and schools. Equally important is to communicate a caring disposition and our commitment that we will do whatever it takes to ensure they and their children feel safe, physically and emotionally, in our classrooms and schools.

As with any kind of interactions, however, we must understand that we are in a position of receiving information that may be confidential or sensitive. When those situations arise, it is our duty and responsibility to immediately consult with appropriate professionals (e.g., school nurse, school administrator, school counselor, school psychologist, social worker) who are trained to guide us through the needed next steps.

Time for Reflection

1. Review Figure 5.1 and create your own invitation for a partnership meeting you might hold to get to know a family.

2. Review Figure 5.2 and revise it to reflect the questions you might ask, making sure they elicit information about a family's strengths you can capitalize on for your classroom instruction (if you are a teacher) or interactions (if you are non-direct instruction staff).

3. Engage in an interview with a family member using the invitation and questions that you crafted. Identify what went well with the activity and what areas you will strengthen to make it better.

Making Frequent Contact with Families

Thus far, this chapter has underscored the importance of getting to know our students and their families. It introduced a partnership meeting format as one of the means for doing this. Whatever we choose to do has to be for the purpose of understanding students' and families' experiences so that we can build relationships and an effective instructional program on behalf of students' success as learners and members of their classroom community and beyond. This should guide our purpose.

As such, we must consider the overall goal of student success as we apply any activity or tool. This is particularly true for the well-being of students living with trauma, violence, and chronic stress. According to Saleebey (1996), families and students experiencing distress may be particularly vulnerable to victimization. Included in this mix is the real complexity of misidentifying students as having disabilities or suspending students when other educational measures would have been much more appropriate. We must also be mindful of English learners, whose learning needs are distinct from students and educators who are native speakers of English. These factors should focus our attention away from looking for what is wrong to a more positive and affirmational approach that acknowledges our students' and their families' strengths. Indeed, when practice focuses on strengths, families and children have been found to greatly benefit (Guo & Tsui, 2010).

Key to building and sustaining strong and empowering family partnerships is frequent and repeated positive contact with families. Let's have a look at our middle school teacher, Alicia Herrick, and how she interacted with families in the past versus what she does now. In the past, she often had students who acted out. For example, on a typical day, when she introduced a lesson, a student might say, "Why do we have to learn this stuff?" When this occurred, Alicia would typically stop class and send the offending student to the school office. Sending students to the office became such a frequent occurrence that during one of her classes, more than a third of her students had been sent out of the room! A significant number of these offenders then received internal or external suspensions. Over time, the same students spent more time out of her class than in it. Many were in danger of failing. She referred many for a special education evaluation. It also meant that every contact with families was about what their children had done wrong. It reached the point where she began to question her professional practice. It also led to her thinking about partnering with families on behalf of their children's education. Following this path, let's look at research findings about using a strengths-based approach with families.

Guiding Principles for a Strengths-Based Partnership Approach with Families

A strengths-based approach is based on the following interdependent guiding principles (Arnold, Walsh, Oldham, & Rapp, 2007):

- All individuals and families possess strengths.
- All individual and family communities possess great resources.
- It's essential to draw from individual and family strengths and self-determination to achieve a set of goals.
- Partnerships are critical.
- Outreach to a family's community is essential.
- All partners and participants are capable of growing, learning, and changing.

Developing a relationship with families in distress can be critical for our students. Personal contact—whether through face-to-face interactions, phone calls, e-mail, or video services such as Skype and FaceTime—can make the difference between being disconnected or connected with our family populations. This is true for families that have experienced violence, as a whole family system can be affected by these circumstances (Rossen & Hull, 2013). We believe that this is also true for any student living in distress.

It is helpful to consider the significance of frequent and positive contact. Thinking of contact in terms of frequency can help greatly. Some of us might be used to contacting families when things are not going well or when they are going very well. If we think of this as a pendulum, we are swinging widely left and right, and never in a slow and steady position. Consider the following questions and how their answers would influence your practice:

- How can I keep a family abreast of what their child is doing well?
- How can I express this even in terms of the smallest celebration of that student?
- How can I support families to draw from their values, assets, and strengths and reflect these back to them?

Alicia initially had a hard time communicating with some families. She had grown accustomed to contacting families when their child was misbehaving or in danger of failing. Once she grew more comfortable with making contacts that were positively oriented, she found that it was much easier to speak about what their child was doing well. She also uses the opportunity to energize the family by valuing and acknowledging the assets and strengths that she has identified through their relationship. As such, Alicia constantly looks for ways to celebrate her students' successes and share them with families. When she does that, she identifies the many qualities and values underlying and sustaining the students' observed behaviors. They are reflected back to the students and their families so they can be part of the students' and the families' *inner wealth* image (Grove & Glasser, 2007; Glasser, 2011). Here are three examples from three different contacts that Alicia made recently. In each, she has observed her students carefully and has made contact with families about a positive detail that she has observed about her students:

- How great it is that [child's name] comes to class on time. She is demonstrating great responsibility!
- It is terrific to see [child's name] participating in class. Today, for example, he volunteered a response to a key question I asked about the Aztecs. He is demonstrating great enthusiasm for learning!
- I appreciate how [child's name] takes time to ask questions about what we are studying. Today, for example, she asked several questions about the poster project that we are creating. She's showing so much curiosity and eagerness to learn more each day!

Alicia also takes the same time to acknowledge the values and qualities she observes in families so she can continuously build and strengthen their personal asset-based account. Here are a few examples:

- *Background information:* Luis has shown inconsistent attendance throughout the year. Alicia has observed that he has not missed a day in the last couple weeks.

  Teacher's positive affirmation to the parent: "Thank you for helping Luis have such excellent attendance lately. I can see how much you value education because you are making sure he is here every day. I'm glad he has not missed a single day of school in the past two weeks. Thank you for being such a responsible and dedicated mother and a great partner in education!"
- *Background information:* Milania is a quiet and hardworking girl under the care of a foster parent. She has attended multiple schools and has experienced several school transfers during the same school year. Her reading skills are far below grade level.

  Teacher's positive affirmation to the foster parent: "Milania comes to school every day with her reading form signed by you. You are a great partner, and I feel I can count on you to help Milania keep developing her reading skills. Thank you for being so helpful. We make a great team!"

- *Background information:* Ms. Alamo is Doran's mother. Alicia was recently informed by Ms. Alamo that she was suffering from a life-threatening illness that was going to require weekly medical visits to receive specialized treatment. These visits were scheduled only in the afternoon and many times were in conflict with Doran's school dismissal time. Ms. Alamo had no one to pick up Doran from the bus stop and take care of him while she was at the appointments. On the days Ms. Alamo had her medical treatment, she notified the school that Doran was going to be absent.

  Teacher's positive affirmation to the parent: "Ms. Alamo, I appreciate you letting me know when Doran is going to be absent because you have nobody to stay with him after school while you are at your weekly medical procedure. I know you are very concerned about Doran missing school, and I will put you in contact with our social worker, who can help you address this situation. Thank you for your honesty and for showing so much responsibility and commitment toward Doran's education. We appreciate that you have put your trust in us."

Sometimes we may have difficulty identifying assets and strengths in others. Consider a student who is chronically absent or tardy, or one who sleeps through class. You may be saying to yourself, "I don't see any personal strengths in this student." If we are committed to looking for and acknowledging strengths in ourselves and others, it is essential to remember that (1) preconceptions and judgments are barriers to developing an understanding of students and their families and (2) our intention is for parents to see us as partners, not as adversaries. Thus, inquiry about the student's or family's situation with an explicit intention to provide support and not criticism will translate into a stronger partnership.

Time for Reflection

1. Drawing from the family contacts that Alicia Herrick made, observe a student that you are concerned about. Create two detailed, positive examples to share with the family in celebration of their child's efforts. Make sure you identify and reflect back the values underlying the observed behaviors.

2. Using Figure 5.2, conduct a partnership meeting with a parent or guardian. Create three examples of your own that acknowledge parents' assets.

Involving Families in Classroom-Based Events

An integrated, positive, strengths-based approach to addressing challenges involves collaboratively exploring the *possibilities* of solutions as opposed to the *impossibilities*. We cannot view our work with students and their families as a solo process that we alone must do. The frequent contacts that we make, for example, can be made much more robust and relevant when we confer with colleagues, other families, students, community members, and other stakeholders to ensure that what we are doing has the best chance of being received positively and with trust. This requires that we look at what is possible when we collaborate to secure solutions.

Classroom-based events are a great means for bringing families together. Let's look at four primary school-family partnership goals for these types of events (Zacarian & Silverstone, 2015). Each is based on our genuine interest to partner with families in mutual support of their children:

- Using community-building events for social purposes.
- Showcasing the curriculum to make learning transparent.
- Drawing on the rich resources of family communities.
- Fostering a shared culture of learning between home and school.

Using Community-Building Events for Social Purposes

Without question, one of the most important elements of ensuring our students' involvement in school is their families' engagement with us (Henderson et al., 2007). Bringing families into school or going to families for a social purpose can do a lot to create positive momentum and trust. Indeed, many of us are seeing the importance of creating experiences that help us get to know families socially. Recently, for example, one of us provided a professional development activity for teachers of students living with trauma, violence, and chronic stress. She asked, "What do you do to get to know the families of your students?" The following are emblematic of the many responses shared:

- We have monthly social gatherings like our art night, music night, and game night.
- I travel with our school counselor to our students' homes.
- I travel to where families go to church so that I can introduce myself to the community.

The first chapter presented research about the distinctions between a mainstream cultural belief in individualism and competition and a minority belief that favors collectivism and relationships as a way of being and acting (Tyler et al., 2008). It also discussed the growing numbers of students and families from underrepresented populations. As such, many of us are seeing the importance of building social relationships and interactions with families. Here is a way of thinking about how we gather families. Think of the typical bake sale in an elementary school. A family from the dominant culture may wish to bake the best cake of all because they come from an independent and competitive culture. A family from a minority culture may prefer baking with a group, as this reflects their collectivist culture. Social gatherings can be ideal places for getting to know and work with families.

However, it is critical to explicitly invite families, welcome them as we would guests in our own home, and explain the routines and activities that will occur so that they may participate the most comfortably. Let's look at one school's art night. You may have many ideas about what this evening looks like, or you may have none. What is critical is to explicitly explain the event to families so that they know what to expect. Figure 5.3 is an invitation to an art night activity from Alicia. It is important to remember that all written communication directed to families needs to be translated into their native language if we are honestly committed to sending a message of inclusion and belonging.

Figure 5.3 | Art Night Invitation

Dear Families,

Your child, [name of student], has been studying early Aztec civilization during our social studies class. We are excited to hold an event to celebrate the type of art that the Aztecs created! During this special night, on [date and time], please come to create figurines such as the ones that were created by the Aztecs. We will provide clay models and clay for this activity. Please come with your child and any family member or friend that you would like to participate in creating your family's special Aztec figurine. Child care and transportation will be available to accommodate families' needs. Please let me know if you will be able to attend and if you plan on using these services.

Thank you very much, and I'm looking forward to seeing you.

Sincerely,

Alicia Herrick

Think about the invitation that Alicia sent. In it, she invites families to an event that celebrates their children's studies through engaging everyone in an art activity. The details of the event involve much more than simply laying out the clay for families to create figurines. She will need to prepare by (1) having people at the door to greet families and take them to the art event location, (2) welcoming families, (3) providing directions and a model for the art creation activity, and (4) creating a closing activity that honors the efforts of all the families. The same holds true for any social family event, whether it is a potluck supper, game night, or any other suggested by families and, more importantly, designed with their input and contribution.

These strategies are relevant not only to our traditional families, but even more to those families who face significant adversities. They are the ones who will benefit greatly from our genuine and caring outreach. Likewise, we will benefit from a trusting collaboration that will enlighten and enrich the way we interact with them.

 Time for Reflection

Plan a classroom-building event for social purposes and respond to the following questions.

1. Describe the type of event that you think would yield the best participation and be most inclusive of your student and family populations.

2. Whom would you include in the planning process?

3. Create an invitation to the event.

4. Describe the steps you would take to ensure that the event is successful from beginning to end.

5. Describe what you would say and do to reflect back the assets and strengths demonstrated by your students' families.

Showcasing the Curriculum to Make Learning Transparent

Curriculum-centered events have great potential for families to celebrate their children's successes in learning the curriculum being studied. They also provide an opportunity for students to show what they have learned. Events such as poetry slams, video productions, and reading and writing publication events can be inspiring spaces that honor students' work and allow families to see and experience what their children have learned. With this as a goal, the possible types of showcase activities are endless. What is important to consider is that they not be competitive, as competition may bring out conflict among students and families and it may not be representative of the diverse families' cultural ways of being, especially those from collectivist cultures.

Alicia wants to share student learning with families. Students work in small groups to create a poster presentation of the art and culture that was created by the Aztecs. Each small group creates a 10-minute presentation about their posters. Families, staff from the middle school, and community members are invited to the poster presentation. To make it as successful as possible, Alicia collaborates with her teammates (who teach English, mathematics, and science) as well as the school's administration, guidance counselors, parent outreach staff, and her alumni from prior years. Everyone assists Alicia in making the event successful. Alumni, staff, and administrators greet families at the door and bring them in small, intimate groups to the classroom. They help the students prepare their presentations. They help Alicia plan two separate poster presentation showcase events to accommodate the various family groups.

 Time for Reflection

Create an event that showcases the curriculum to make learning transparent, and respond to the following questions.

1. Describe the event you would hold.

2. Whom would you include in the planning process?

3. Create an invitation to the event.

4. Describe the steps you would take to ensure that the event is successful from beginning to end.

5. Describe what you would say and do to reflect back the assets and strengths demonstrated by your students' families.

Drawing on the Rich Resources of Family Communities

It is critical to support families in distress by acknowledging and valuing their strengths as active members in their children's education. One question that we should be asking ourselves as we explore this concept more deeply is: "What can I do to continuously involve students and their families in my classroom or school?"

Saleebey (2000) highlights the idea that asking families about the skills, interests, and talents that they might share can be important for getting to know families that have experienced high levels of distress. Following that line of thinking, let's look at one of the questions that we asked in Figure 5.2, to help us identify families' strengths: What special talents or interests would you consider sharing with the students in [name of child's] class or with students' families?

Some families are comfortable with this question because they are deeply familiar and comfortable with their children's school as an institution or have had successful experiences in school themselves and can respond to this question with ease. Others may not feel that same sense of familiarity and comfort. Still others may be experiencing high levels of stress and may not yet feel they have the capacity to respond to this question. Families experiencing distress may need our support and help identifying their unique strengths, abilities, and values to share. So where one set of family members may respond readily and with ease to the question, others may not for a range of reasons. For example, some low-income families might miss the richness of their experience and knowledge and how they can contribute to their children's education if they are overwhelmed with socioeconomic challenges.

Unlike a survey that asks a fixed set of questions to be completed within a fixed time period, relationship building is dynamic and full of possibilities as we create more and more opportunities for families to collaborate with us. When talking about expanding parental roles in schools and building on their strengths, Valencia (2010) alludes to the concept of *funds of knowledge* addressed by Gonzáles and colleagues (2005) in their research with low-income Mexican immigrant parents. They state:

> Funds of knowledge refers to those historically developed and accumulated strategies (skills, abilities, ideas, and practices) or bodies of knowledge that are essential to a household's functioning and well-being. . . . A key finding from our research is that these funds of knowledge are abundant and diverse; they may include information about, for example, farming and animal husbandry, associated with households' rural origins, or knowledge about construction and building, related to urban occupations; or knowledge about many other matters, such as trade, business, and finance on both sides of the U.S.–Mexico border. (pp. 91–92)

Our students' families have rich funds of knowledge that we can tap into to create rich lessons and strong school-family relationships. It is only when we reach out in our capacity as learners that we are able to identify, acknowledge, and value their assets and strengths. One helpful way to think about family engagement in our classrooms is to consider the different types of family events that we can hold. Another is to consider that when we all feel a true sense of partnership with families, even those in distress, we are much more likely to feel and act through a collaborative lens of respect.

Consider this example of a way that Alicia draws from the rich resources of her students' families. During an interview with some of the families with undocumented experiences, she learns that one of the parents is an artist and is familiar with the type of art that was created during the Aztec era. As Alicia plans for the art night event described earlier, she asks this father to share with families how he would create a figurine. With an interpreter, the father comes to the event and carefully shows families how to create a figurine out of clay.

Fostering a Shared Culture of Learning Between Home and School

Renowned sociologist Joyce Epstein (1986) completed one of the most comprehensive and seminal surveys on parents' perceptions about their children's school. Parents from a range of educational experiences, from those with no high school diploma to those with graduate degrees, responded. One of the findings was that parents felt that they didn't know how to help their children with schoolwork and that this feeling of not knowing how to help intensified during their children's secondary years. More current research shows that this finding continues to be an important concern for families (Epstein et al., 2009; Henderson et al., 2007).

It is essential to support families being involved in their children's learning. However, we may be inclined to think that many families, including those in distress, may not be familiar or may have not had experience in the subject matters that we teach and/or how we teach it. Without making assumptions (one of our premises), we should explore this further by reaching out to families. If it is found that a family is open to learning about a specific topic, we can then proceed to create this particular shared experience. The following options help support a shared culture of learning bewteen home and school.

- *Student-family learning extension interactions.* It can be very helpful to include families in the work of learning by assigning students tasks to do with families. For young learners, this can be a simple assignment of having students take a book home and read it to a family member or friend to support their learning. Included in this plan can be a card or sheet with suggested questions that parents can ask their child as they are reading. Indeed, all subject matters can include this type of event, whereby students engage in a task that requires interaction with someone about what they are learning. Examples of this include a 6th grade biology teacher who is doing a unit of study on food safety as it relates to germs, bacteria, and fungi. He asks students to interview a family member or friend about whether it is safe to eat something that you dropped on the floor if you pick it up in five seconds. Another example is a high school biology teacher who asks her students to explain the process of cell division to a family member or friend and come to class with questions that they were asked about the process or challenges that they had in presenting the information.
- *Family curriculum events.* Events such as a math night can be a critical venue to make what is occurring in school more familiar to families. Families are invited to attend an event, and the event itself is a time to share with families what can be done at home to support their children's learning. One example of this is a 3rd grade teacher who invited parents in for a multiplication event. During the event, parents and their children created math games that could be played at home to support their children learning times tables.

It is important to remember that these events can be held at any place in the community that is suitable for parents. In addition, to accommodate families' needs, increase participation, and remove any existing barriers, take into account logistics about transportation and child care services.

Using the ideas discussed in this chapter to build a strengths-based partnership approach to foster family engagement supports students in being more involved and empowered in their own education. Similar to the interventions we put in place to accommodate the needs of our second language learners that also happen to benefit native speakers of English, these recommendations are suitable for all families. The next chapter discusses creating a school-based team approach that is inclusive of students and families living with trauma, violence, and chronic stress and the teachers, support and administrative staff, and other school-based stakeholders who serve them.

Infusing a Strengths-Based Approach Across a School

Just as schools are composed of many different people, including students, families, teachers, specialists, and administrators, it takes everyone working together to build and maintain a community where every person feels a sense of belonging and of being safe, valued, and competent. This is especially important for students and families living with trauma, violence, and chronic stress, as is thinking carefully and collaboratively about how we work with such students and their families, as well as with each other. This chapter uses the terms *collaborative, collective,* and *team* and *school team* to mean the interactions that occur when we work with one or more teachers, administrators, specialists, and support and non-support staff in pairs, small groups, or as a whole school community on behalf of students and families living with trauma, violence, and chronic stress.

In Chapter 5, we met Alicia Herrick, a middle school teacher who attempted to work on her own in support of her students. If you recall, she would gather up her own children's old clothing and bring it to the students she felt were the most in need. This gesture did not work very well. She would also send students out of her classroom when they "acted out," figuring that it was best to take care of these behaviors. That, too, did not work very well. It wasn't until she decided to reach out to and work with the school's social worker that she implemented a more positive and successful teaching approach. In this chapter, we look at the positive effects of using a strengths-based team approach—and there are many! We will do this by exploring the following questions:

- Why is it critical to use a strengths-based team approach?
- Why is it crucial to scale up collaborative interactions between and among students, their families, and the school community?
- Why is it critical to create an inclusive strengths-based team based on a school's unique circumstances and existing strengths?

Why Is It Critical to Use a Strengths-Based Team Approach?

There are some general reasons for using a team approach. An obvious one is that we can learn much more from each other and widen our circle of understanding, approaches, and strategies when we work with others as opposed to working alone. The underlying principle is that there is always so much more we can do on behalf of students and families when we work collaboratively. This is especially true for the unique circumstances of our diverse students and families living under extremely adverse conditions. It is also true when addressing our need to remain emotionally strong and healthy amid the demands and challenges of working with and serving students and families who live with trauma, violence, and chronic stress.

As important as it is to understand the value of a team approach, it is critical that it be based on affirmation and energizing students to reach their potential. Also, those who make up our school communities may not know whom to ask for support and what services or supports to tap into. Take, for example, a teacher who learns in passing that one of her students witnessed his father's and brother's deaths during a civil war in his home country. While the teacher understands this reality, she is not quite sure whether and even when it is appropriate to work with someone in school on this student's behalf and who that person should be. Let's look at another example. In this case, a different teacher learns that a group of students has collectively experienced a horrific traumatic event, like a shooting in their home neighborhood. As in the first example, the teacher is not sure what appropriate steps to take. Another example is Alicia Herrick. She took steps that she believed would work, only to find that they didn't. Yet another example is a teacher who takes a number of steps that he finds effective with most students but less effective with students and families that he has little familiarity or professional experience with. In addition, every school community includes staff engaged in nonteaching roles, such as custodians, coaches, security staff, office staff, and others. They, too, are often deeply engaged with and concerned about working with students living with trauma, violence, and chronic stress and have varying degrees of confidence and support in doing so. Each of these examples, and the countless ones that we have not presented, points to the need for using a team approach that is positive and based on affirmation and empowerment. Let's begin by looking at the possibilities of collaboration in our own contexts.

This book began with a finding from the National Survey of Children's Health (Data Resource Center for Child and Adolescent Health, 2014) that half of the students in the United States have experienced or are experiencing trauma, violence, and chronic stress. One of the key reasons for using a team approach is this reality. That is, in each of our schools, a wide range of traumatic and violent experiences are affecting some students and their families to varying degrees and can also affect the professionals in our school communities who are working on their behalf. According to Cole and colleagues (2005), every school, in its own special way, can and must support students experiencing trauma, violence, and chronic stress. They cite findings from Masten and Coatsworth (1998) and the National Child Traumatic Stress Network (2008) about the importance of partnering with families, strengthening students' relationships with adults, and supporting students in their social-emotional growth so they may flourish in and out of school. Also, they emphasize the importance of knowing that every school can and should use its own resources and talents to create lasting supports for every student living with these circumstances.

Why Is It Crucial to Scale Up Collaborative Interactions Between and Among Students, Their Families, and the School Community?

While the suggestions made by Cole and colleagues (2005) are critical, we must look closely at how we can scale up the amount of positive, caring, and meaningful interactions that we have with students, their parents/guardians, their family community, and the school community to develop the most effective, appropriate, and lasting responses. Chapter 1 described the various circles of interactions that occur during a child's development. This chapter

Figure 6.1 | Circles of Interactions Within a School Community

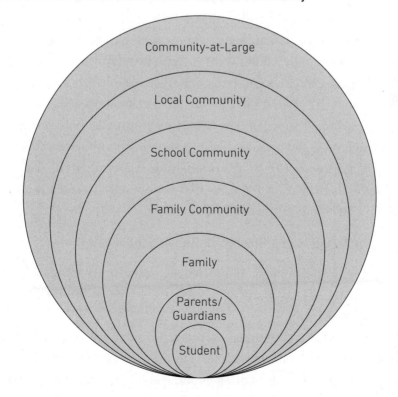

highlights four of these (see Figure 6.1) to look more closely at the interactions that can occur when we use a team approach.

Indeed, the types of responses that Cole and colleagues (2005) advocate can occur most effectively when these four circles of interaction are fully supported, encouraged, and energized. The four circles encompass the students, their parents/guardians, their family community, and the school community (including students' peers, teachers, administrators, support professionals, and others).

Each of us has something powerful to contribute to the school team. Indeed, one person can and does have the power to influence others positively when that person is encouraged and feels valued for doing so. One of us, for example, provided professional development in a small city in New Jersey. The training included elementary and secondary subject matter teachers, administrators, special education teachers, ESL and bilingual teachers, guidance counselors, and security staff. The latter group, the security staff, had many ideas to share about how they show students that they are cared for and cared about. Officer James, one of the security officers in attendance, said, "I make it my business to get to know the students. I know their names. I try to get to know their families and friends. I don't want them to do anything but succeed here."

According to Cole and colleagues (2005), a whole school approach can make a tremendous difference in the education of students living with trauma, violence, and chronic stress, and every school is "uniquely positioned to help children reach their potential" (p. 44). Just as a school in New Jersey would include its security staff in its comprehensive response efforts, each school must develop its own team response that is unique to its circumstances and population and base it on three characteristics.

Three Characteristics of a Strengths-Based School Team

1. It taps into and honors, acknowledges, and affirms students', families', and our own strengths so that we can enact the type of meaningful partnerships that are needed.

2. It looks carefully at the circles of interactions that are available to students so that we may draw from these as fully as possible as we support students to become the best version of themselves and reach their academic potential.

3. It is steadfast in its resolve to empower and energize students to reach their academic and overall human potential.

Let's have a look at Tyler, a 7th grade student enrolled in the school that Officer James works at, to illustrate the possibilities of tapping into these circles of interactions to create a whole school framework. In this chapter, we follow Tyler through the course of his first year in middle school.

 ## Take a Closer Look: Tyler (Example 1)

Officer James has gotten to know Tyler and has learned some important information about him. Tyler lives with his mother and younger brother in his aunt and uncle's home. His parents are both addicted to opiates, and his father is currently in jail serving a sentence for breaking into a pharmacy where he had planned to steal drugs. During the past year, Tyler and his brother were separated into two different foster homes while their father was incarcerated and their mother was placed in an inpatient drug treatment facility. Before Tyler went into foster care, he lived in a number of homeless shelters with his mother and brother. He has missed and continues to miss a lot of school. Officer James worries that Tyler will fail school and possibly drop out because he is so far behind. Each time they speak, Officer James's goal is to have a caring conversation with him. He has found that Tyler is quite friendly and open to speaking with him. He recently learned that Tyler enjoys playing video games.

Giving Everyone a Voice

What greatly helps anyone involved in a team effort is the belief that individual voices are valued, honored, and acknowledged. Indeed, it is the first characteristic and is emblematic of a comprehensive team approach. In school settings, this occurs when we, as educators, continuously model and affirm that everyone's contributions matter. This type of reciprocal affirmation modeling is akin to what Daniel Pink (2009) found in his review of 50 years of behavioral sciences research about motivation. In his review, he found that motivation requires the following elements:

- It requires a sense of knowing that each of us has something important to contribute and that our individual creativity in making these contributions will be acknowledged and honored.
- It requires that each of us is given precise and accurate feedback targeted to helping us further our efforts to improve what we do.
- It requires that we know that our work is regarded as valuable and meaningful by others.

Indeed, when Pink looked closely at various successful institutions, he found that these three characteristics were always present. Motivation hinges on our being given the opportunity to contribute actively and receiving affirmation of our contributions in this effort.

 Time for Reflection

1. Reread example 1 about Tyler. What are five words you found yourself using to describe Tyler's or his family's experiences?

2. Use the following system to categorize the descriptive words you identified in question 1 and your reason for this categorization.

Descriptive word about the student or family	Positive word that affirms the student's or family's strengths	Neutral word that objectively states facts	Word that is used negatively to identify or describe a problem (behavior, circumstance, etc.)
1.			
2.			
3.			
4.			
5.			

Providing Precise Feedback to Scale Up a Positive Strengths-Based Approach

Perhaps you found that you used positive words to describe Tyler or that you used mostly neutral words that described facts about him. Or maybe you found that you used mostly words that negatively identify a circumstance that Tyler experienced. Every time we use positive words to provide precise feedback (i.e., reflecting back individuals' values and attributes), we increase the chances of tapping into our students' potential and having them exhibit positive behavior more often. It might relate to a type of positive interaction that we have with students, families, and each other; a teaching strategy; a programming idea or practice; or something else. Whatever it is, when we use precise positive, affirming, and energizing feedback, it benefits the recipient as well as the provider. When these types of interactions become generalized and practiced by everyone in the school community, teaming up on behalf of our students and families becomes easier. Consequently, teaming up allows us to create a comprehensive approach that is much more targeted to students and families living with trauma, violence, and chronic stress.

 Time for Reflection

1. Revisit example 1 about Tyler. Considering his uniqueness, identify something he can contribute to the class and what kind of verbal affirmation you would use to acknowledge and honor his qualities and values that allowed him to make these contributions.

2. What areas do you wish you had more information about to respond to question 1?

3. Tyler is enrolling in your school or classroom. What type of positive affirmation might you initially give him to acknowledge his enrollment and reflect back some of his attributes that will make his experience in your school or classroom a positive one?

4. How can you support Tyler and his classmates in seeing Tyler, as we should see all students, as a valuable and meaningful member of the school community?

 Time for Reflection

You are Officer James. Using Figure 6.2, identify the person or people you would meet with and fill in the blank circles to create a team to support Tyler's social-emotional and academic success that fits your particular context.

Figure 6.2 | Tyler's Classroom and Family Community

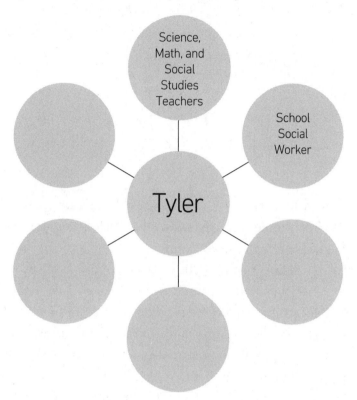

1. What would your purpose be in working with this team (e.g., improving Tyler's attendance, getting a mentor for him, arranging for him to receive academic tutoring, encouraging him to attend after-school programming)? What assets will the team draw from to achieve this purpose?

2. What two or three statements will the team make that will reflect back to Tyler the strengths that have been identified (e.g., "We see your passion for playing video games, and we think you might like to try our after-school gaming club where everyone can learn from your knowledge")?

In the previous reflection activity, we looked at Figure 6.2 to determine a possible person or people who will work with Tyler. In order to create a real sense of collaboration and to make him feel valued and competent, we give Tyler a seat at the discussion table. His voice and opinions are as valuable and important as those of any other team member. Let's say that we all determine that Tyler would greatly benefit from working with all of his teachers and the school's social worker to support him in a number of ways (e.g., attendance, academic skills, participation in after-school activities). If we consider the value of Tyler working with them, we might argue reasonably that each of these people is critical to his social, emotional, and academic well-being. At the same time, we also have to consider two groups who are not on the list: Tyler's peers and his family. Earlier in this book we discussed the importance of partnerships and relationships. What might happen if we tapped into all of the possible resources that are available to Tyler? Surely this includes many more people than his teachers and the social worker. Indeed, when Tyler is in school, he spends a good amount of the day with his peers. And when he is home, he is with his mother, brother, aunt, and uncle.

So when we work on behalf of our students, we have to think carefully about the positive possibilities that we can provide. For example, Tyler loves playing video games, and when Officer James learns this, he works from Tyler's interests and strengths and includes Tyler's voice. He discusses how they will

Figure 6.3 | Tyler's Widening Classroom, School, and Family Community

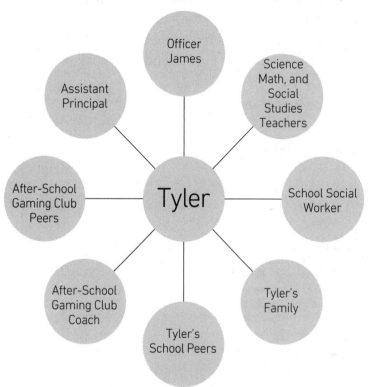

support Tyler to join the after-school gaming club. As with any team that works with students living with trauma, violence, and chronic stress, the goal of Tyler's team is to broaden and strengthen the circles of positive interactions that Tyler is exposed to. Figure 6.3 depicts the interactions that the team, including Tyler, designs for him.

As important as it is to think of the possible circles of positive interactions that can help in supporting students living with adversity, it is equally important for us to think carefully and reflectively about our interactions. While most of us have the best intentions in our work, it is critical that we routinely engage in self- and collaborative reflection about our collective work. This calls for us to look closely at our individual and collective use of a strengths-based mindset. Using a strengths-based approach that highlights and reflects the values and qualities people bring with them decreases the chance that negativity will leak into the relationships we are trying to develop. This approach contributes to the uncovering of our students' potential.

 Time for Reflection

Rate yourself on the following scale:

	Most of the Time	Some of the Time	Rarely
When I work with others on behalf of students, I routinely begin by highlighting the students' or families' strengths.			
When I work with others on behalf of students and their families, I routinely begin with what I perceive as the identified problem.			

If you are engaged in a school community with a team, rate yourself in the following collective activity after meeting about a student or family living with trauma, violence, and chronic stress.

 Time for Reflection

Rate your team on the following scale:

	Most of the Time	Some of the Time	Rarely
When working with a school-based team on behalf of students and families, we devote meeting time to identifying and highlighting students' and families' strengths.			
When working with a school-based team on behalf of students and families, we spend meeting time identifying and highlighting what is perceived as the students' or families' problem.			

Transforming Our Professional Practice by Intentionally Using Affirmation

Tyler's story objectively illustrates what has occurred in his life. Many of us, not surprisingly, may find ourselves discussing our students' or families' problems with our team of colleagues. Identifying problems might be what we naturally do. As discussed in Chapter 5, we may tend to do this by unconsciously following an older, more traditional model of naming the problem, as opposed to identifying and affirming students' and families' strengths. As a result, some conversations with others lean toward what we perceive as the negative aspects of what students are experiencing or have experienced. Let's apply this to Tyler. If we are asked to talk about him, we might start a conversation with how sad it is that he has lived in a homeless shelter, how behind he is in school, the many gaps that he has in education, and so forth. Further, because one of us might start the conversation with what we perceive is emblematic of his and his family's problems, others may find themselves continuing this type of conversation.

Indeed, when we speak with others in groups, we engage in conversation according to what we hear. Bailey (1993) studied this phenomenon and found that people tend to be honored or acknowledged based on how they connect what they have heard and comment on it in conversation. It might be in the form of a personal reference such as, "I hear what you are saying," where we refer to the person who has spoken. It might also be an ideational reference signaling that we hear another person by repeating a short phrase that they stated, such as, "Yeah, a lot of limited schooling." We might also keep the thread of conversation going by adhering to or connecting the same train of thought as prior speakers. And we might also make a backchannel remark, a verbal signal such as "Yes" or "Uh-huh" to show that we are listening (Bailey, 1993; Willett, Bailey, Jeannot, & Zacarian, 1998). It's also important to remember, as discussed in earlier chapters, that the great majority of people have good intentions toward others, and when we persist on talking about our students' adversities, it is mainly a reflection of concern and care for those we perceive as less fortunate. Some of the values and qualities underlying this behavior are caring, compassion, dedication, empathy, and responsibility.

Let's return to Tyler. A team of six people is having a professional conversation about him. They include Officer James, the school's social worker, the assistant principal, and Tyler's English, science, and social studies teachers. This is the first time they have gathered together to discuss Tyler. The following is the opening segment of their conversation.

 Take a Closer Look: Team Discussion About Tyler (Example 2)

Officer James:	Tyler has lived in a lot of homeless shelters and foster homes. I have no idea how many!
Science teacher:	Yeah.
English teacher:	But he has missed so much school and is so far behind. He just cannot keep up in class. Like, today, we are supposed to be reading the book *I Am Malala* to connect with what you are doing in social studies [points to social studies teacher], and I am not sure he can do it.
Social studies teacher:	Yeah, he has missed so much.
Social worker:	Yes, I hear you, and it is very sad.
Assistant principal:	We have so many students like Tyler.

 Time for Reflection

Can you identify the values and attributes underlying these professionals' statements about Tyler in example 2? Let's say that we asked the team to complete the individual and collaborative reflection activities from earlier in the chapter. How do you think they would answer?

Imagining yourself as a member of Tyler's team, rate yourself and the team on the following scale:

	Most of the Time	Some of the Time	Rarely
When I work with others on behalf of students, I routinely begin by highlighting the students' or families' strengths.			
When I work with others on behalf of students and their families, I routinely begin with what I perceive as the identified problem.			
When working with a school-based team on behalf of students and families, we devote meeting time to identifying and highlighting students' and families' strengths.			
When working with a school-based team on behalf of students and families, we spend meeting time identifying and highlighting what is perceived as the students' or families' problem.			

More than likely, we each would say that few, if any, spoke about Tyler's strengths. Rather, the conversation focused on his perceived problems. To move to a positive, strengths-based individual *and* team approach means that we must be guided by the following questions. Otherwise, we might form teams with good intentions and miss the amazing possibilities of drawing from students' and families' strengths.

- How can we begin with and work from students' and families' strengths?
- How would these strengths be acknowledged and reflected back to one another throughout our school and culture?
- How can administrators, teachers, families, students, and others support a strengths-based approach?
- What is the role of professional development in supporting a strengths-based approach in all of the teams we form?

Expanding the Use of Positive Affirmations: From Small Groups to Whole School

We must learn to collectively look first to our students' and families' strengths. This doesn't mean that we ignore what is happening. Rather, it is a means to ensure our collective focus on affirmation. Let's go back to Tyler to see an example of this type of collective thinking. His team meets with the goal of developing strategies that will support Tyler's school attendance, socializing, and academic performance. The following is the opening segment of their conversation.

 Take a Closer Look: Group Discussion About Tyler (Example 3)

English teacher:	Although Tyler has lived in a lot of different home situations and has missed a significant amount of schooling, I have observed that he comes to class every day on time, is working hard to make friends with his classmates, and has agreed to meet with me after school and during study hall to support his learning. He's just a trooper! He's really showing responsibility and a commitment to learning. I am really excited to work with him and welcome input and ideas about what we have each found to be successful with him.
Science teacher:	Yeah, I have noticed the same in my class with regard to punctuality and interaction with peers. He is showing great willingness to learn!
English teacher:	We are reading *I Am Malala* in class. It's the one that we selected to match what you are studying in social studies [points to colleague].

Social studies teacher:	Yeah, it's a great book. I am looking for ways to help Tyler and my other students get more interested in what's been happening in South Asia and am glad we are meeting and that I can count on you all! Thank you for helping me create more engaging lessons.
Social worker:	So it sounds like Tyler is showing great responsibility by coming to class on time, is committed and eager to learn, and is showing determination in building connections with his peers.
Officer James:	When I speak with Tyler, he always tells me how much he enjoys gaming. It would be great for us to get him in our after-school gaming club so he can keep cultivating his interests in technology.

 Time for Reflection

1. You are Tyler's mathematics teacher. Refer back to example 2 and add a next sentence to the team's discussion.

2. You are Tyler's mathematics teacher. Refer back to example 3 and add a next sentence to the team's discussion.

3. Describe three differences that you noticed between your responses to examples 2 and 3.

Perhaps you found yourself writing an extension to example 2 that kept the focus on the many traumas Tyler has experienced in his life, whereas example 3 supported a more positive, strengths-based focus that looks at who Tyler is as a person. While acknowledging our students' and families' lived experiences is necessary, finding the values and assets hidden behind adversities provides us with the tools to grow people's potential. It is equally important to routinely take time to reflect on a team's work. For example, the team that is working with Tyler would periodically complete the same reflection activity that we did earlier to ensure that their work is focused on Tyler's strengths and assets.

 Time for Reflection

Let's say that Tyler joins the after-school gaming club at his school and you are his club coach. You are asked to reflect on the meeting that was just held. Rate yourself on the following scale.

	Most of the Time	Some of the Time	Rarely
When working with a school-based team on behalf of students and families, we devote meeting time to identifying and highlighting students' and families' strengths.			
When working with a school-based team on behalf of students and families, we spend meeting time identifying and highlighting what is perceived as the students' or families' problem.			

Having Tyler as a valued participant in this group also adds a unique element that we need to consider. Adult interactions serve as a model for Tyler to learn from, so it is very important for adults to communicate frequently and intentionally about their values and qualities even under difficult situations.

Let's reflect on the same meeting, but this time Tyler is an active member in it.

1. You are Tyler's English teacher. Refer back to example 3 and restate the affirmation so you are now communicating it directly to Tyler in person.

2. You are the school social worker. Refer back to example 3 and restate the affirmation so you are now communicating it directly to Tyler in person.

3. You are Officer James. Refer back to example 3 and restate the affirmation so you are now communicating it directly to Tyler in person.

Why Is It Critical to Create an Inclusive Strengths-Based Team Based on a School's Unique Circumstances and Strengths?

Regardless of where we work, the teams that we build on behalf of students and families living with trauma, violence, and chronic stress must include as broad a range of members as possible to ensure that a student's whole school experience is positive socially, emotionally, and academically. This might seem challenging, especially when some of our schools have programs and activities (e.g., special education, English language instruction) that separate students as well as educators from each other instead of bringing them together. This programming often requires that students leave the general classroom to receive individual or small-group instruction or support from specialists who rarely, if ever, work with the general population and often work in isolation.

School and district leaders play a key role in making sure that using a strengths-based approach with students living with adversity (as well as with the overall student population) is part of the core of each school's vision and mission and not an add-on or a box to be checked. This functions best when school leaders, including principals, assistant principals, department or curriculum leaders, and district program administrators work in close partnership with the school community to benefit students' positive social and emotional well-being and academic success.

An example of this type of comprehensive approach occurred in Kansas City, Missouri. In Chapter 3, we introduced you to Chris Homiak and his student Javier. We described the strategies Chris used to identify and acknowledge Javier's individual and family assets. We also learned that Chris teamed up with his school's social worker, his district's director of English language learner services, and others to support Javier and his family. Let's have a look at the activities they engaged in, and let's identify and acknowledge the hidden assets and qualities this family possesses. You may want to go back and refer to Figure 2.1 (p. 30) for a list of values and qualities worth acknowledging, if needed.

Take a Closer Look: Description of Supports Javier Was Given (Example 4)

Javier's family was buoyed by several support structures offered by our building and district. Our building's social worker worked tirelessly with the family, connecting them with utilities assistance and helping with transitions to different shelters. The district's English Language Learner Department director and Spanish interpreter worked closely with the social worker, helping Javier's Spanish-speaking mother with paperwork, critical communications, and crisis management. These support services maintained open, collaborative communication throughout the year and served as a strong safety net for Javier's personal and academic growth, in spite of the challenge of continued transitions in his living situation.

Time for Reflection

Pretend you are Chris Homiak and are participating in a team meeting about Javier.

1. What underlying values or qualities can you identify in Javier's mother?

2. What would you say to this family to acknowledge the attributes you have identified? Be very specific in your description.

Take a Closer Look: Supports Javier Was Given (Example 5)

School personnel even provided foster care for Javier's beloved cat, which enabled him to focus on schoolwork when the family was evicted from their apartment and moved to the first in a series of homeless shelters.

Time for Reflection

Pretend you are Chris Homiak and are participating in a team meeting about Javier.

1. What underlying values or qualities can you identify in Javier's behavior?

2. What values and attributes does Javier possess that might stop him from making poor choices?

3. What would you say to Javier to acknowledge the attributes you have identified? Be very specific in your description. Make sure you label the values so Javier can incorporate them into his understanding of his own strengths and can draw from these in all that he does.

These reflection activities required us to interact using asset-based language. When we work in teams, it is imperative to have positive, asset-based interactions and verbal communication with students and families living with trauma, violence, and chronic stress. Such interaction should be second nature to our work. Let's look at the team that worked on Javier's and his family's behalf using an additional reflection activity.

 Time for Reflection

1. Reflecting on the circles of interaction that were activated to support Javier and his family (Figure 6.4), describe the positive actions that you believe most contributed to his success based on the uniqueness of his school.

Figure 6.4 | Javier's Circles of Interaction

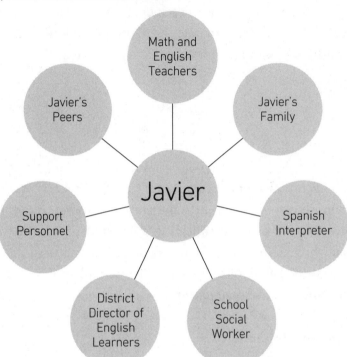

2. Consider your school context (or a school that you worked in or attended) and its unique circumstances. What circles of interaction do you believe could be included to ensure the social, emotional, and academic success of students living with trauma, violence, and chronic stress?

Widening Our Circle to Create a Whole School Approach

In this chapter, we have looked at the approaches that were used in a classroom and a school on behalf of an individual student. Cole and colleagues (2005) discuss the importance of integrating whatever we do into what is already occurring in a school community, while at the same time ensuring that we meet the social, emotional, and academic needs of students. We see this type of self-reflection and evaluation as a recursive process (see Figure 6.5) in which we are always evaluating the success of what we are doing to be sure that we are constantly strengthening our practices.

Figure 6.5 | Recursive Review of Policies and Practices for Students Living with Trauma, Violence, and Chronic Stress

Under federal laws and regulations, school leaders, regardless of their work, have an important role in ensuring that the confidentiality of students and families is protected under the Family Educational Rights and Privacy Act (U.S. Department of Education, 2015). Picture a sign posted on an elevator in a hospital that says, "We protect the privacy of our patients." What we do to ensure the privacy of our students and parents is akin to the care that the hospital staff takes to ensure that this occurs for all of their patients. However, some of us have observed school personnel erroneously shying away from sharing crucial information that would guide a more informed approach with students and families living with trauma, violence, and chronic stress. If students and families would benefit from the sharing of information, then school personnel should make every effort to obtain written permission from parents/authorized caregivers to do so.

In addition, school leaders have an important role to play to ensure that the school's policies and practices take into account the various and diverse needs of its students and families living with adversity. Let's say, as a hypothetical example, that Javier's school has a long-standing policy that students with more than six absences in a semester can receive no higher grade than *B* unless the student's family furnishes a documented medical excuse. This policy does not take into account the countless examples of students living with trauma, violence, and chronic stress, including Javier, who missed many days of school moving from one homeless shelter to the next. A comprehensive review of policies and practices and how they are applied to students living with these phenomena can make them much more appropriate.

Throughout this chapter, we have seen how we can provide a team approach based on the unique circumstances and strengths of our individual schools. School and district leaders, teachers, support staff, and others play unique and important roles in ensuring that their school's assets are identified and tapped into on behalf of students' social, emotional, and academic success. For example, we saw how Tyler's and Javier's education was supported in unique and distinct ways based on the circumstances of their individual schools.

Oftentimes, however, we find that we don't have the professional experience needed in a range of areas. Let's say, for example, that we have little familiarity working with students living in homeless shelters. School administrators are key to helping identify and implement the necessary professional development activities. Figure 6.6 is intended to help us identify what is already occurring in our schools and what will occur through professional development initiatives.

The next chapter will move from using a school-based team approach to looking at the urgency and possibilities for building school/district–community partnerships that help us understand, identify, and capitalize on assets in the community. We will also look at ways to create effective and continuous networking and collaborative partnerships with community-based agencies serving students and families living with trauma, violence, and chronic stress using our strengths-based approach.

Figure 6.6 | Infusing a Strengths-Based Team Approach into a School

1. Read the following descriptions.
2. Check the left column for procedures that your school/district already does.
3. Check one of the columns on the right for procedures that will occur in 30, 60, or 90 days. In the space below the procedure, identify the specific steps to be taken to accomplish this procedure and the person(s) responsible.
4. Add two to four additional procedures that will occur in 30, 60, or 90 days, and include the person responsible or specific steps to be taken to accomplish these additional procedures.

Occurs	Procedures	Will occur in 30 days	Will occur in 60 days	Will occur in 90 days
	Meetings about students and families living with trauma, violence, and chronic stress focus on identifying their strengths and assets and reflecting these to them.			
Action Steps:				
Person(s) Responsible:				

(Figure continues on next page)

Figure 6.6 | **Infusing a Strengths-Based Team Approach into a School** *(continued)*

Occurs	Procedures	Will occur in 30 days	Will occur in 60 days	Will occur in 90 days
	The unique circles of possible interactions for students living with trauma, violence, and chronic stress are routinely identified, honored, acknowledged, and valued to ensure students' social, emotional, and academic success.			
Action Steps: Person(s) Responsible:				
	The action steps taken on behalf of each student living with trauma, violence, and chronic stress are based on the student's and our school's unique strengths.			
Action Steps: Person(s) Responsible:				

(Figure continues on next page)

Figure 6.6 | Infusing a Strengths-Based Team Approach into a School *(continued)*

Occurs	Procedures	Will occur in 30 days	Will occur in 60 days	Will occur in 90 days
	We routinely examine the social, emotional, and academic growth of students living with adversity to identify the professional development that is needed for instructional and non-instructional staff and other stakeholders. Examples of tools to use are student surveys, parent/caregiver surveys, and staff surveys.			
Action Steps:				
Person(s) Responsible:				
	Additional Procedure:			
Action Steps:				
Person(s) Responsible:				

Capitalizing on Community Assets to Build Partnerships

Alone we can do so little; together we can do so much.

—Helen Keller

At Wolfe Street Academy, a preK–5 school in Baltimore, Maryland, a packed room of students, parents, staff, administrators, and community liaisons gather in the cafeteria each morning before school starts. They discuss the various activities that are occurring at the school—and there are many. They also take time to publicly acknowledge the accomplishments of students, staff, and community members. At the end of the meeting, families are welcome to pick up the abundant bags of groceries that have been generously donated from local markets and farms. Some families linger after their children have gone to class to meet with fellow parents and partners from the school and community to draw from each other's assets and ideas (WETA Public Broadcasting, 2017a).

A decade ago, Wolfe Street Academy was one of the lowest-performing schools in Baltimore. Now, it's one of the city's top-performing schools. One of the major reasons for its success, according to Principal Mark Gaither, is the wide array of partnerships that it has made with the community, providing students and families with health care, social services, family supports, and much more. These partnerships did not happen overnight. Indeed, it took many years and many lessons learned to move from failing to highly successful. An example is found in the story of a tragedy that occurred in a community not far from Wolfe Street Academy: the death of Deamonte Driver, a 12-year-old student who died of a brain abscess from what should have been an easily treatable toothache. According to an article in the *Washington Post,* a "routine $80 tooth extraction might have saved him. If his mother had been insured. If his family had not lost its Medicaid. If Medicaid dentists weren't so hard to find" (Otto, 2007, para. 2). The efforts of Representative Elijah Cummings of Maryland helped secure a multifaceted approach to meet the needs of the state's children ("Cummings Introduces Children's Dental Bill," 2009). Wolfe Street Academy's comprehensive preventative dental care, other services, and educational programming exemplify these actions.

Thus far, this book has addressed four core essentials for students living with trauma, violence, and chronic stress: that they feel safe, valued, a sense of belonging, and competent. Until this point, we have focused on what happens *inside* our schools to ensure that the four essentials are met on a regular and consistent basis. In this chapter, we look *outside* the school to see how students' success in school and beyond can be increased significantly—and even dramatically—when we carefully and intentionally consider what can occur when we work with community partners to recognize the goodness in our students, families, and communities and seek lasting solutions that tap into their strengths. As we will see in this chapter, there is much that we can do on behalf of students living with these circumstances when we partner with our communities to identify, create, and implement actions that bring out students' and families' assets and address their needs and desires.

This chapter examines the importance of identifying, building, and sustaining school/district–community partnerships using a strengths-based approach. We look at how we can engage in understanding, identifying, integrating, aligning, and capitalizing on the many assets that exist in the communities where we work. In addition, we focus on the possibilities of effective and continuous networking and collaborative partnerships with community-based agencies, services, and others that work on behalf of students and families living with trauma, violence, and chronic stress.

Throughout this book, we have discussed the importance of developing positive, asset-based interactions with and on behalf of students and, equally important, that students have with others. Figure 7.1 displays the circles of critical interactions and partnerships. Students' well-being is directly connected to our collectively working together on their behalf. The National Child Traumatic Stress Network (2008) cites numerous research findings that the more we interact with students, their parents/guardians, their family community, the school community, the local community, and beyond, the more comprehensive and integrated our work can

Figure 7.1 | Circles of Interactions

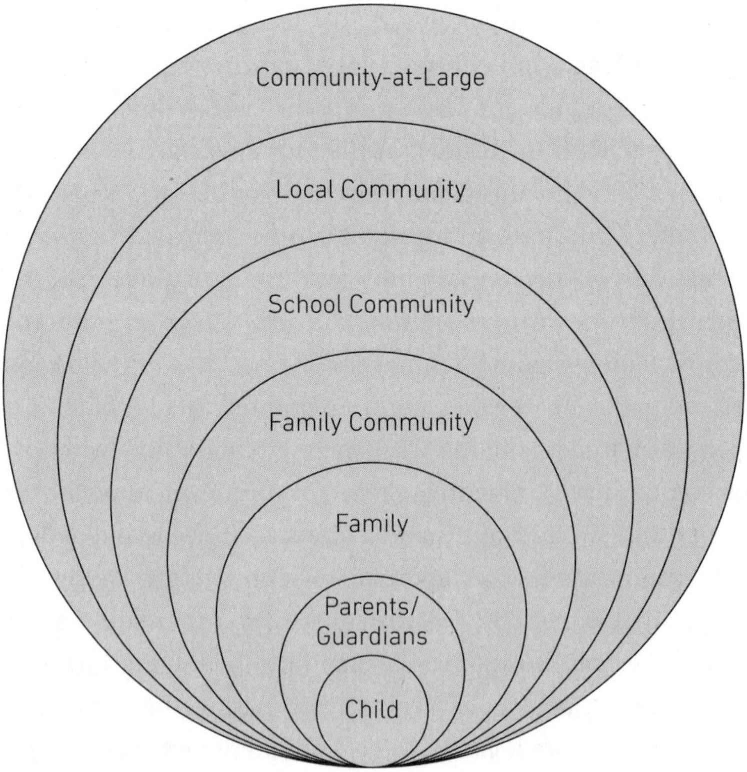

Community-at-Large

Local Community

School Community

Family Community

Family

Parents/
Guardians

Child

be and the more successful students are in school. But we also know that it is the type and quality of interactions that directly influence outcomes. We constantly have tremendous opportunities to positively influence others when our interactions are guided by a genuine desire and a conscious intention to look for and acknowledge the human value in each person we interact with.

This chapter shows the importance of being intentional in working with these circles of interactions and the steps we need to take to build the types of school–community partnerships that nurture our students' capacities and assets. The chapter also draws from various examples from Wolfe Street Academy and elsewhere to show how these ideas work in action.

Expanding to an Asset-Based Approach with School–Community Partners

Many professional organizations—including ASCD, the association that published this book—recognize the value of school–community partnerships. Indeed, ASCD and others use the term *whole child* to describe the comprehensive considerations, inputs, and actions that are needed to ensure that a child is "healthy, safe, engaged, supported, and challenged" (ASCD, 2017a, para. 2). The cornerstone of the ASCD Whole Child approach is that a child's well-being and development can only be achieved when educators, families, community members, and policymakers work as partners on behalf of students. This is of particular relevance when we work on behalf of students and families living with trauma, violence, and chronic stress.

The Whole School, Whole Community, Whole Child (WSCC) Model looks at various sectors of a child's development (e.g., medical, dental, nutritional, social) to ensure that the child's needs and desires (e.g., enrichment activities such as a chess or dance club) are met. This approach takes into account two important realities: (1) many sectors serve the same children, and (2) schools are in the best position to support and align the coordinated efforts of all involved. While some might say that our schools are not in the business of doing more than educating children, ASCD and a number of other professional organizations and scholars recognize the need to expand the scope of services on behalf of the students and families we serve. They understand the critical importance of addressing the barriers that can interfere with optimal development and supporting student learning. The following components are identified by the WSCC (ASCD, 2017b):

- Physical education and physical activity
- Nutrition environment and services
- Health services
- Counseling, psychological, and social services
- Social and emotional climate
- Physical environment
- Employee wellness
- Family engagement
- Community involvement

 Time for Reflection

1. Discuss why you believe all nine of these components are critical for a whole child approach.

2. Use an example from your own context or experience to describe the application of a specific component with students living with trauma, violence, and chronic stress.

Another part of the ASCD Whole Child approach is that each of our schools is uniquely positioned to understand the needs and desires of our students and to create lasting partnerships with our local communities and beyond. For example, Wolfe Street Academy had students, like Deamonte, who came to school with significant dental problems. In a video interview, Wolfe Street's school–community coordinator, Connie Phelps Bozek, recounts what it was like in the past when a good portion of students lacked access to dental services, as evidenced by the large number of students with dental issues (WETA Public Broadcasting, 2017a). Although we recognize this as a challenge, it is when we look for the resources and assets in a community that we are able to move forward and address challenges more effectively. As a result, Wolfe Street Academy partnered with the University of Maryland's School of Dentistry to create and implement a comprehensive dental program for its students. It includes dental screenings and care and classes for parents/guardians to increase their knowledge of dental hygiene and nutrition practices. It also involves older students helping younger students during dental screenings and care. The Wolfe Street Academy and University of Maryland School of Dentistry staff understood that when students' dental care needs are met, students are much more able to concentrate on learning, as opposed to coping with pain. School staff continuously take time to identify community resources and cultivate relationships with those who are able to support student learning. This approach draws from students' and families' assets; in this case, their abilities to be receptive, to cooperate, and to join efforts with school and community members working on a common goal.

Finding Strengths-Based Characteristics in Whole Child Programs

Let's look at two examples of school districts that tapped into the assets of their communities and, in particular, the resource of nonprofit institutions to address the challenges of students living with trauma, violence, and chronic stress. The first is the partnership that the Kansas City, Missouri, schools designed and implemented with the Truman Medical Center. The second is the partnership between two public school districts in New York and a private mental health organization.

Take a Closer Look: A School District and a Medical Center Address Trauma Together

In Kansas City, an implementation model called Trauma Sensitive Schools (TSS) was developed and implemented in 2013 by Truman Medical Center Behavioral Health. This medical center began by helping teachers understand the characteristics of trauma and develop responses that would honor and acknowledge students, while also supporting them in being successful learners in the classroom (Molly Ticknor, personal communication, January 31, 2017; Zacarian & Lukens, 2016). Between 2013 and 2017, more than 2,500 Kansas City Public School staff were trained in the model, with four teams being identified as the strategic implementers of pilot programs for the TSS initiative. Let's look at one of the schools to see some of the features of the school–community partnership that was created.

Garfield Elementary School is a K–6 school in a diverse part of Kansas City. Of its 500 students, 97 percent receive free or reduced-price lunch, and half are English learners that represent more than 40 language groups, 20 countries of origin, and refugee experiences. The staff at Garfield Elementary wanted to identify ways that would help them understand and draw from students' and families' cultural assets and strengths and that would best support students to cope with traumatic experiences. Working closely with their school-based partners, the consultants from Truman Medical Center developed personalized plans that empowered students to be in control of their emotions (Molly Ticknor, personal communication, January 31, 2017).

Garfield Elementary is also using a sanctuary model concept known as the *community meeting*, which includes a daily ritual that can be adapted to any environment or classroom. The students and staff are asked three questions: How are you are feeling today? What is your goal today? Who can you ask for help? The goal of the meeting and questions is to create a classroom norm and culture of safety, trust, and personal responsibility. In a video titled *New Americans Class, Community Circle Time* (Paden-Dowdell, 2016), we can see these plans in action.

The curriculum includes how to support students to strengthen their understanding of stressors that might trigger a negative response, ways to identify and use a more positive response, and strategies for making these a way of being and acting as students learn to use them with frequency. Included here is an image that shows one of the strategies students were taught from teachers trained by Truman Medical Center staff to help students better understand coping strategies. The positive side of this is that it empowers students to feel capable of recognizing their feelings and developing options to manage them. When they use the phrase "I can . . ." the underlying message that is communicated is that students are capable, competent individuals in control of their own emotions (see Figure 7.2).

Figure 7.2 | Example of an Empowering Strategy

The results of Garfield Elementary School's partnership with Truman Medical Center were dramatic. It resulted in a more positive school climate, as indicated by a significant reduction of disciplinary referrals and out-of-school suspensions. These successful outcomes are the result of the positive possibilities of the partnership between the two institutions and the careful planning and implementation that occurred (Zacarian & Lukens, 2016).

Our second example begins with three questions that were developed to help transform teachers' practice. As we will see, this example includes some of the same content as our Kansas City example.

Take a Closer Look: Public–Private Partnership to Create Trauma-Responsive Schools

In New York, a three-year professional development initiative in partnership with the Andrus Foundation was implemented in a suburban public school district that had a significant number of students and families experiencing high levels of stress and trauma. The goals of its trainers, educators Eileen Santiago and Joanna Ferrara and social worker Sarah Yanosy, were for teachers to promote students' social-emotional well-being, growth, and learning using an assets-based approach. To do this, the Andrus Foundation implemented a trauma-responsive program, which it refers to as a *sanctuary model,* to help teachers develop trauma-informed practices in schools.

A large part of this professional development supports teachers and other professionals who work with students living with trauma, violence, and chronic stress to recognize their own triggers and traumas and to learn a specialized set of strategies to respond effectively. According to Santiago, Yanosy, Ferrara, and Harrison (2016) the sanctuary philosophy hypothesizes that to become a trauma-informed school, there must be an essential change in the way students who exhibit challenging behaviors are viewed. Discussions about students should not begin with "what is wrong with the child." Rather, a fundamental principle should be a dialogue centered on "what has happened to you" and supporting students living with trauma, violence, and chronic stress to rescript their individual responses to trauma when faced with comparable incidents in the future.

To empower students to recognize their feelings and manage their emotions, teachers were trained to start the school day using a community meeting format that routinely began by asking students to respond to three questions:

- How are you feeling?
- What is your goal for today?
- Who can you ask for help?

According to Santiago and colleagues (2016), starting the day with a community meeting helps to create a safe space for students to share feelings, set goals, and build relationships. It also establishes a predictable, protective environment that equips students with tools to continue to develop a positive self-image. Further, they claim that it also gives teachers opportunities to gauge the emotional tenor of their class.

Designing a Systematic Approach to Building Community Partnerships

The previous chapter discussed the importance of teaming together on behalf of our work with students living with trauma, violence, and chronic stress. It included an example of a school-based team that was created on behalf of one student, Tyler. If you recall, they identified Tyler's strengths and assets and drew from these to support him as a learner and member of the classroom community.

The same type of identification and mapping holds true when working with community partners. That is, the same ideology of drawing from the strengths and assets of partners *and* students and families is applied in school–community partnerships. To do this, we have to think of the partnerships that we create as inclusive, dynamic, and evolving to meet the unique assets and also the challenges our changing student populations face that prevent them from demonstrating those assets. For example, while the content of the professional development used by the trainers in Kansas City and

New York might be similar, they both needed to work in close collaboration with the school partners to make sure that what they did was tailored to and responded well to the students and families they serve.

Leverage Community Resources to Promote the Four Essentials

When we look outside the school and reach out to our communities and stakeholders, it is important to consider the external resources that will best support our work of promoting relationships that foster a sense of safety, belonging, competency, and human value. This is particularly important as we prepare to partner with organizations that will provide services to our students and families living with trauma, violence, and chronic stress. We need to be particularly attentive to how these partners perceive our focal population (i.e., that they are using an asset-based approach and view students and families through this lens). We also have to pay close attention to how we perceive the community where the school is located, always keeping our asset-based spectacles on and looking through them.

The Asset-Based Community Development (ABCD) approach offers a way of working with communities that focuses on their strengths and assets. John McKnight and Jody Kretzmann, founders of the ABCD Institute at Northwestern University, challenged the usage of any model based on the deficiencies of neighborhoods and communities (i.e., what is wrong) as opposed to the inherent strengths and assets of all communities as an essential basis for sustainable revitalization. Among these assets (DePaul University, 2017) are

- The skills of local residents.
- The power of local associations.
- The resources of public, private, and nonprofit institutions.
- The physical infrastructure and space in a community.
- The economic resources and potential of local places.
- The local history and culture of a neighborhood.

Schools have tremendous opportunities to draw from the invaluable resources of their communities and engage in positive and productive relationships with them. It usually starts with asset mapping, a process that identifies all the assets listed above that are unique to a particular neighborhood. This could be conducted by a team of people that represent different stakeholders (e.g., parents, teachers, community members) with the purpose of identifying resources that support the school mission and ongoing efforts to reach higher levels of student personal and academic achievement.

When schools reach out to identified resources in the community (e.g., institutions, associations, religious entities, nonprofit organizations, volunteer groups), they are usually received with open arms and a genuine desire to support students and families. After all, efforts directed toward improving the quality of life in a community benefit all who live and work in it. Take, for example, a school where one of us used to work in Hartford, Connecticut. The school principal sought out and developed a relationship with a community stakeholder who committed to creating and sustaining a school-based program to address the needs of students who had no access to comprehensive eye exams, including eyeglasses. Students were referred to the vision clinic when routine vision screening conducted by the school raised concerns about their vision. Parents were always involved in the process and joined with the clinic in reinforcing the importance and benefits of good vision for adequate learning.

Move Beyond Identified Needs

Partnerships should be about more than merely addressing identified needs in schools; they should also, and most importantly, be about enhancing and supporting all the gifts and assets that people bring with them (e.g., potential, curiosity, leadership skills, compassionate feelings, thirst for learning, positive disposition, desire for justice) and capitalizing on them for the community's well-being. From local businesses providing students with internship and job shadowing experiences to community centers serving as recruitment sites for new students, there are endless possibilities for communities and schools to partner with each other. When we focus on building these partnerships, we are also addressing any challenges and barriers that may prevent students, families, and schools from using their assets. Challenges and barriers become opportunities for school–community resources to let assets and strengths shine throughout.

 Time for Reflection

1. Make a list of some of the resources in your (school) community that benefit families and youth.

2. Think about ways your school can benefit from a partnership with them.

3. Think about ways any of these organizations, associations, or other entities can benefit from partnering with your school.

Mapping Out a Response That Draws from Strengths and Assets

Figure 7.3 shows the steps to consider when developing a school–community partnership response.

Let's use this resource to look at the partnership that occurred between Wolfe Street Academy and the University of Maryland School of Dentistry as a means to understand the steps for mapping a community partnership.

Figure 7.3 | Steps for Mapping School–Community Partnerships

1. Create a group of passionate individuals who will team up to identify community resources and map community strengths.

2. Assign a school–community liaison to facilitate partnerships.

3. Identify ways that potential school–community partners can contribute to the school and ways that the school can contribute to the community.

4. Identify ways that community resources can provide support to the school to enhance assets and address challenges.

Create a Group of Passionate Individuals Who Will Team Up to Identify Community Resources and Map Community Strengths

Recognizing people's abilities and skills and their passion for making connections is necessary to create a team that will be committed to asset mapping. This team must acknowledge that lasting solutions come from within the community and that they need to look first to the residents' gifts and skills, as well as the assets of the physical community (Chrzanowski, Rans, & Thompson, 2010).

For example, various staff at Wolfe Street Academy knew that they needed to address the challenges of students who desperately needed dental care, families who did not have access to or were unfamiliar with these services, and families who did not have sufficient income to cover the cost. They also knew that this was particularly true for students from undocumented and uninsured families (WETA Public Broadcasting, 2017b). Finding out what resources they had in the community that could provide guidance and direct support to address these challenges was important, as this was affecting students' ability to let their assets shine fully.

This first important step of identifying a challenge cannot be minimized. At the same time, while some of us may know the various barriers our students and families face, we may not be sure how to address these, whether it is "our job" to do so, and whom to go to so that we can ensure these needs are met. We may also trip over each other in our genuine commitment to support our students and families. For example, let's say we know that one of our students is in dental pain and we call our own dentist to see if she will help. Unbeknownst to us, another teacher, counselor, or non-support staff member recognizes the same need in the same student and begins making contacts on his own to help. Creating a simple system that is known and understood by all can assist with this situation. It also allows people to show their care and concern, as well as their empathetic values. Additionally, it presents another opportunity for all of us to recognize these values and acknowledge them in each other.

Wolfe Street Academy principal Mark Gaither (personal communication, November 10, 2016) states that the most important aspect of identifying a challenge is listening to students and families. He also says that initially he relied on one person as his and the staff's go-to person. While this was helpful, he realized some important lessons after she left. First, it's critical to build many partnerships with others and to draw from everyone's strengths. Also, it's equally important to share in the process of securing long-lasting relationships and not create a response that is solely dependent on one person.

This leads to the second important step: identifying a school–community liaison or, where applicable, a district–community liaison who, supported by this committed group of people, will create a clear process for collaboration and facilitate the partnerships that are needed.

Assign a School–Community Liaison to Facilitate Partnerships

A point person in each of our schools or districts best ensures that the school–community partnerships and activities that we create are seamless, aligned, coordinated, and effective. In some schools, this position may be full-time. In others, it may be one of many roles assigned to existing staff, such as a school social worker, nurse, or guidance counselor. And in still other schools, district-based staff, such as the director of pupil personnel, are assigned this role. Wolfe Street Academy employs a full-time school community coordinator, Connie Phelps Bozek, who noted some of the common characteristics of a school–community liaison (WETA Public Broadcasting, 2017a):

- Knows school's teachers, parents/guardians, community members, and leaders.
- Identifies resources (values, qualities, knowledge, etc.) that students, families, and school personnel already possess that can support and address any barriers other people are facing and that may be preventing them from displaying their own inherent qualities (e.g., a parent who is familiar with a community's medical and dental services and can support a family to gain access to these; a student who can support peers' dental hygiene practices).
- Identifies or helps identify resources to enhance students' learning and any barriers that prevent students from displaying their assets.
- Understands the school–community liaison as a project-based role, with each project seeking enhancement of school assets and a solution to any learning challenges.

- Works with the community to match its talents and resources with the talents, values, desires, and challenges of students and families living with trauma, violence, and chronic stress.
- Collaboratively develops solutions and examines the actions needed to address these solutions to ensure that they are working and that steps are taken to strengthen them when needed.

Identify Ways That Potential School–Community Partners Can Contribute to the School and Ways That the School Can Contribute to the Community

One of the most critical activities is securing community partners that do two things:

- Respond to an identified need, such as a challenge that needs to be addressed, as well as the need to cultivate students' assets and strengths.
- Base their collaboration on mutual interests.

For a partnership to work, there has to be something in it for everyone so that it is not a lopsided relationship. For example, Wolfe Street Academy's Principal Gaither stated that when the school began seeking community partners, they knew instinctively that they had to "insulate their students and their families" from being taken advantage of. An example he volunteered was a potential partnership with a law firm that wanted its interns to mentor Wolfe Street Academy's students. The law firm's plan was for Wolfe Street's students to leave school and travel to the firm to eat lunch during the interns' short lunch break. Let's apply this example to the rule that a partnership must respond to an identified need. Although for some it may have sounded like a good mentorship opportunity, the logistics only seemed to benefit the potential mentors and not the students or school community. School–community partnerships must first and foremost respond to an identified challenge for our target audience, students living with trauma, violence, and chronic stress. In doing so, the positive aspects of these partnerships result in addressing challenges *and* supporting students to achieve their potential.

According to Chrzanowski and colleagues (2010), effective partnerships benefit both sides: "Community organizations, residents, and businesses benefit from strong relationships with schools that ultimately support the entire community" (p. 14). While the school benefits from the community support and resources, the school's assets in turn are of major benefit to the community. Here are some of the benefits mentioned by Chrzanowski and colleagues:

- Schools represent a central location to share information with community residents.
- Schools have facilities that can be used as meeting spaces, community conference centers, and sites for community events.
- Students serve as volunteers and interns in community-based organizations and businesses and strengthen school protective factors. (p. 14)

Wolfe Street Academy's partnership with the University of Maryland School of Dentistry is a fine example of one that benefited both institutions. It began, more than a decade ago, with teachers noticing a growing number of students complaining of being in dental pain. Through the school–community coordinator's connection to the University of Maryland, she contacted their dentistry program and asked if it would help. This resulted in dental interns, under the direction of Clemencia Vargas, coming to the school to do screenings and support students who needed dental care. The partnership also includes dental health education programs for parents/guardians. In addition, it involves Wolfe Street Academy's students acting as assistants. As a result, the partnership allowed both institutions' student populations to continue developing and enhancing their skills and abilities while also feeling good about it.

Identify Ways That Community Resources Can Provide Support to the School That Will Enhance Assets and Address Challenges

Although we purposefully intend not to dwell on the negative, we are not oblivious to the challenges or barriers that schools and communities face. These, too, are important to consider and address. For example, one of the biggest challenges that Wolfe Street Academy has faced is helping students from undocumented families successfully obtain dental care. Dr. Vargas shares the reasons for these barriers to participation:

> Dental insurance has been demonstrated to be fundamental for dental care, especially among low-income children. So the fact that most low-income children are covered by Medicaid is one tremendous step towards oral health, but . . . there's a group of children who are not eligible for Medicaid insurance. And those are the children from undocumented families, children, usually, who were born in another country and come here without their papers in order. These children can't apply for Medicaid. They have access to education, they have access to some health services, but they don't have access to Medicaid, and so they don't have access to dental care. (WETA Public Broadcasting, 2017b)

Identifying Responses to Potential and Known Barriers

As important as it is to identify a challenge, it is critical to continuously persevere to find lasting solutions. Here is what Vargas says about addressing a known barrier:

> Through the years, we have been raising funds to be able to see these children and get them some discounts at our school of dentistry, but it's a very serious problem that has to be addressed from a more general perspective. (WETA Public Broadcasting, 2017b)

This statement could paralyze some people and prevent them from seeing the many opportunities and the potential to unite efforts and talents to address such a challenge. It is important to remember that one of the most powerful elements of partnerships is, literally, the power of numbers. The more partners we can assemble, the greater our chances of addressing a challenge. At the same time, the more partners that there are, the more need there is for aligning the work. We will come back to this later in this chapter when we look at partnerships working in harmony with each other.

Draw from the Assets and Strengths of Students and Families

An additional critical element of any partnership is the way we draw from the assets and strengths of students and families living with trauma, violence, and chronic stress. In the past, such students and families may have been marginalized or treated as having no assets or strengths, but a solid partnership is one in which the school and community understand the value and possibilities of all people. Regardless of their backgrounds and life experiences, we must be relentless in our efforts to ensure that all students, particularly those living with adversity, feel safe, valued, a sense of belonging, and competent. This requires that we intentionally seek ways for students and families to be active partners with us. Here is an example, from Vargas, of one of the ways in which Wolfe Street Academy and the University of Maryland School of Dentistry engage students as partners and assets in their dental programming.

> The older children already come here and talk to us, and they are helpers, and they want to—like you saw today, the girl holding the light—she wanted to be part of it. And so [she] could understand and she'd talk about molars. So those are wonderful stories and make dentistry . . . more accessible to the children. And maybe they will think about becoming dentists. You never know. (WETA Public Broadcasting, 2017b)

Designing Asset-Based Community Partnerships

The type of community resources that partner with schools should vary according to the mission of the school, the assets they would like to enhance and promote, and any identified challenges.

Plan Partnerships

Focusing partnerships on our students' and families' assets and strengths has been found to lead to the most successful outcomes (National Child Traumatic Stress Network, 2008). Experts on disaster-related trauma (Gurwitch, Pfefferbaum, Montgomery, Klomp, & Reissman, 2007) state that the act of building community partnerships is akin to the type of preparation that one does to ready for a marathon. We would never go out and run more than 20 miles without first taking time to plan the run and then actually practice running over and over again in all kinds of changing weather conditions. This would be followed with scaling up our runs, beginning with a short distance and building more and more distance as we prepare. Similarly, it is critical to think carefully about who we include in partnerships that are most likely to be successful with our youth, families, and schools.

Include Families as Critical Partners

The first and critical partners in our school community are parents/guardians and students. According to the National Child Traumatic Stress Network (2008), parents/guardians should always be included in working with us to build school–community partnerships. One of the core reasons that this should be a mainstay in any school–community partnership work is the overwhelming research that shows it to improve outcomes for students *and* families. There are also other benefits:

- Increased participation of youth and families from diverse cultural perspectives strengthens the relevance and cultural competence of the partnership.
- It strengthens a sense of ownership and empowerment.
- Ongoing input from youth and families enables partners to continually improve.
- It helps to increase public awareness about an identified need and services.
- Youth and families can be powerful agents for spreading the word about services to others who need help. They can also serve as wonderful mentors and examples to their peers. (adapted from National Child Traumatic Stress Network, 2008, pp. 11–12)

Understand That Community Partnerships Take Time

Our second critical partners are our communities. What is helpful in designing school–community partnerships is supporting our community partners in identifying each other's strengths, so that we are sure to tap into these when addressing an identified challenge in a way that is energizing and empowering for everyone involved. Building a partnership with the community requires them to see that they are change agents because of the energy and relationship that they bring. The National Child Traumatic Stress Network (2008) suggests that we start small with any community partner, doing only a handful of activities initially to ensure that they are manageable and can be quickly strengthened where needed. The National Child Traumatic Stress Network has also found that partnerships tend to build over time when partners see and experience successes. This parallels what Wolfe Street's principal, school–community coordinator, and representatives from the University of Maryland School of Dentist noted over time. It comes from the adage, "Build from your strengths and successes."

Design Goals

The National Child Traumatic Stress Network (2008, p. 15) also provides suggestions for designing the goals for any partnership:

- Collaboratively determine the goals and objectives to focus on.
- Create only a few activities so that they are manageable to implement and analyze.
- When there is more than one goal, set priorities in terms of what will occur first, second, and so forth.
- Create a timeline for implementing each priority and examining its success.
- Continuously assess the resources being used to carry out the plan. Seek help when more resources are needed.
- Begin small, but begin. Make youth and family involvement a priority to achieve buy-in from stakeholders and to keep moving forward.

It is always helpful to use a tool that helps us examine our school–community partnership activities. Figure 7.4 is intended for this purpose.

Ensure That the Partners Work in Harmony

At this point, we understand the value of school–community partnerships. Realistically, schools and districts have the capacity to build a wide range of partnerships with various agencies, services, institutions, and individuals that work on behalf of students and families. As we expand our partnerships, it

Figure 7.4 | Designing School–Community Partnerships

School/District _____

Identified Assets/Strengths: _____

Identified Challenges/Opportunities: _____

School/District Liaison Partner and Team

School Liaison Name: _____ Position _____

School Team Members (including staff, families, and students)

Name _____ Position _____

Name _____ Position _____

Name _____ Position _____

Name _____ Position _____

Partner Institution_____

Institution's Liaison Name:_____ Position _____

Partner Team Members

Name _____ Position _____

Name _____ Position _____

Name _____ Position _____

Name _____ Position _____

Goal 1: _____

Activities in order of priority	Date activity will begin	Date activity will be assessed
1.		
2.		
3.		

Goal 2: _____

Activities in order of priority	Date activity will begin	Date activity will be assessed
1.		
2.		
3.		

(Figure continues on next page)

Figure 7.4 | Designing School–Community Partnerships *(continued)*

Goal 3: _____

Activities in order of priority	Date activity will begin	Date activity will be assessed
1.		
2.		
3.		

becomes increasingly important that all of the partners work in harmony with each other. We distinguish between coordinating services and making sure that we work in harmony with each other in our efforts to address challenges and barriers to learning that students experience. Consider the work of a choir conductor. The conductor can coordinate the soprano, alto, and bass sections so that everyone knows their part and can carry the tune, or the conductor can support the sections to work together to create a perfect harmony with their singing partners. The first conductor is akin to a pot that's quickly filled with high-quality ingredients and ends up with flavors that seem to overpower each other. The second conductor is akin to the same pot of high-quality ingredients that are slowly and carefully blended together to make a savory soup creation.

We have to avoid an overreliance on thinking that more is better, or that doing a lot all at once is better than providing partners with much-needed time to work in sync with each other and benefit from each other's coordinated strengths, assets, and efforts. As we address challenges to learning, it is critically important to consistently gather partners together to ensure that we are doing the following:

- Promoting the success of students and the active participation of families.
- Employing as many sectors as we can to ensure the comprehensive well-being of our students.
- Directly addressing areas to be enhanced or challenges that prevent our focal population from freely demonstrating their assets, thus negatively affecting their learning.

- Working as seamlessly as possible to ensure that services are not fragmented.

As we do this, there are two important questions to continuously ask ourselves:

- What are we doing to reflect our students', families', schools', and communities' values and strengths?
- What are we doing to address any challenges that prevent them from demonstrating these?

When we take into account all of the possibilities for school–community partnerships, the potential for ensuring that all students living with trauma, violence, and chronic stress flourish in school and beyond can become a reality. It calls for us to draw from our students', families', schools', and communities' strengths and assets, as well as ours, to carefully design and implement a strong and beautiful tapestry of opportunities.

References

Adelman, H. S., & Taylor, L. (2013). Addressing trauma and other barriers to learning and teaching: Developing a comprehensive system of intervention. In E. Rossen & R. Hull (Eds.), *Supporting and educating traumatized students: A guide for school-based professionals* (pp. 265–286). New York: Oxford University Press.

American Psychological Association. (2017). Undocumented Americans. Retrieved from http://www.apa.org/topics/immigration/undocumented-video.aspx

Arnold, E. M., Walsh, A. K., Oldham, M. S., & Rapp, C. A. (2007). Strengths-based case management: Implementation with high-risk youth. *Families in Society: The Journal of Contemporary Social Service, 88*(1), 86–94.

ASCD. (2017a). Whole child. Retrieved from http://www.ascd.org/whole-child.aspx

ASCD. (2017b). Whole school, whole community, whole child. Retrieved from http://www.ascd.org/programs/learning-and-health/wscc-model.aspx

ASCD & Centers for Disease Control and Prevention. (2014). *Whole school, whole community, whole child.* Alexandria, VA: ASCD. Retrieved from http://www.ascd.org/ASCD/pdf/siteASCD/publications/wholechild/wscc-a-collaborative-approach.pdf

Bailey, F. M. (1993). *Voice in collaborative learning: An ethnographic study of a second language methods course* (Doctoral dissertation). Available from ProQuest Dissertations and Theses database. (UMI No. 9408253)

Benson, J. (2016). The power of positive regard. *Educational Leadership, 73*(9), 22–26. Retrieved from http://www.ascd.org/publications/educational-leadership/jun16/vol73/num09/The-Power-of-Positive-Regard.aspx

Bernard, M., & Newell, E. P. (2013). Students affected by neglect. In E. Rossen & R. Hull (Eds.), *Supporting and educating traumatized students: A guide for school-based professionals* (pp. 203–217). New York: Oxford University Press.

Biswas-Dienera, R., Kashdan, T. B., & Gurpal, M. (2011). A dynamic approach to psychological strength development and intervention. *Journal of Positive Psychology, 6*(2), 106–118.

Blaustein, M. E. (2013). Childhood trauma and a framework for intervention. In E. Rossen & R. Hull (Eds.), *Supporting and educating traumatized students: A guide for school-based professionals* (pp. 3–22). New York: Oxford University Press.

Bransford, J., Darling-Hammond, L., & LePage, P. (2005). Introduction. In L. Darling-Hammond & J. Bransford (Eds.), *Preparing teachers for a changing world: What teachers should know and be able to do* (pp. 1–40). New York: John Wiley & Sons.

Brown, J. L., Roderick, T., Lantieri, L., & Aber, J. L. (2004). *Building academic success on social and emotional learning: What does the research say?* New York: Teachers College.

Charney, R. C. (2002). *Teaching children to care: Classroom management for ethical and academic growth, K–8.* Greenfield, MA: Northeast Foundation for Children.

Chrzanowski, D., Rans, S., & Thompson, R. (2010). *Building mutually-beneficial relationships between schools and communities: The role of a connector.* Chicago: ABCD Institute.

Cohen, E. G. (1984). The desegregated school: Problems in status power and interethnic climate. In N. M. Miller & M. B. Brewer (Eds.), *Groups in contact: The psychology of desegregation* (pp. 77–95). New York: Harcourt Brace Jovanovich.

Cohen, E. G., & Lotan, R. A. (2003). Equity in heterogeneous classrooms. In J. Banks & C. Banks (Eds.), *Handbook of multicultural education* (2nd ed.). New York: Teachers College Press.

Cohen, E. G., & Lotan, R. (2014). *Designing groupwork: Strategies for the heterogeneous classroom* (10th ed.). New York: Teachers College Press.

Cole, S. E., Eisner, A., Gregory, M., & Ristuccia, J. (2013). *Helping traumatized children to learn 2: Creating and advocating for trauma-sensitive schools.* Boston: Massachusetts Advocates for Children.

Cole, S. E., Greenwald O'Brien, J., Gadd, M. G., Ristuccia, J., Wallace, D. L., & Gregory, M. (2005). *Helping traumatized children to learn: Supportive school environments for children traumatized by family violence.* Boston: Massachusetts Advocates for Children.

Collaborative for Academic, Social, and Emotional Learning. (2016). Examples. Retrieved from http://www.casel.org/examples-page-sel-in-action

Craig, S. E. (2008). *Reaching and teaching children who hurt: Strategies for your classroom.* Baltimore: Paul H. Brookes.

Craig, S. E. (2016). *Trauma-sensitive schools: Learning communities transforming children's lives, K–5.* New York: Teachers College Press.

Cummings introduces children's dental bill. (2009, January 13). Retrieved from https://cummings.house.gov/media-center/press-releases/cummings-introduces-childrens-dental-bill

Darling-Hammond, L., & Rothman, R. (2015). *Teaching in the flat world: Learning from high performing systems.* New York: Teachers College Press.

Data Resource Center for Child and Adolescent Health. (2011/2012). National Survey of Children's Health. Retrieved from http://www.childhealthdata.org/docs/drc/aces-data-brief_version-1-0.pdf

DePaul University. (2017). ABCD Institute. Retrieved from https://resources.depaul.edu/abcd-institute/Pages/default.aspx

Dweck, C. (2006). *Mindset: The new psychology of success.* New York: Ballantine Books.

Early, T. J. (2001). Measures for practice with families from a strengths perspective. *Families in Society: The Journal of Contemporary Social Services, 82*(3), 225–232. doi:10.1606/1044-3894.235

Epstein, J. L. (1986). Parents' reactions to teachers' practices of parent involvement. *Elementary School Journal, 86,* 277–294.

Epstein, J. L. (2001). *School, family, and community partnerships: Preparing educators and improving schools.* Boulder, CO: Westview Press.

Epstein, J. (2011). *School, family, and community partnerships: Preparing educators and improving schools* (2nd ed.). Boulder, CO: Westview Press.

Epstein, J. L., Sanders, M. G., Sheldon, S. B., Simon, B. S., Salinas, K. C., Jasorn, N. R., . . . Williams, K. J. (2009). *School, family, and community partnerships: Your handbook for action* (3rd ed.). Thousand Oaks, CA: Corwin.

Everly, G. S., & Firestone, R. M. (2013). Lessons for developing resilience. In E. Rossen & R. Hull (Eds.), *Supporting and educating traumatized students: A guide for school-based professionals* (pp. 287–298). New York: Oxford University Press.

Felitti, V. J., Anda, R. F., Nordenberg, D., Williamson, D. F., Spitz, A. M., Edwards, V., . . . Marks, J. S. (1998). The relationship of childhood abuse and household dysfunction to many of the leading causes of death in adults: The Adverse Childhood Experiences (ACE) study. *American Journal of Preventative Medicine, 14,* 245–258.

Fisher, D. (2015). *Effective use of the gradual release of responsibility model.* Retrieved from https://www.researchgate.net/publication/266351394_Effective_Use_of_the_Gradual_Release_of_Responsibility_Model_The_Gradual_Release_of_Responsibility_Model

Fisher, D., & Frey, N. (2008). *Better learning through structured teaching: A framework for the gradual release of responsibility.* Alexandria, VA: ASCD.

Fisher, D., & Frey, N. (2013). *Better learning through structured teaching: A framework for the gradual release of responsibility* (2nd ed.). Alexandria, VA: ASCD.

Floyd, D. T., & McKenna, L. (2003). National youth organizations in the United States: Contributions to civil society. In D. Wertlieb, F. Jacobs, & R. M. Lerner (Eds.), *Promoting positive youth and family development: Community systems, citizenship, and civil society: Vol. 3. Handbook of applied developmental science: Promoting positive child, adolescent, and family development through research, policies, and programs* (pp. 11–26). Thousand Oaks, CA: Sage.

Frey, N., & Fisher, D. (2006). *Language arts workshop: Purposeful reading and writing instruction.* Upper Saddle River, NJ: Merrill Education.

García, S. B., & Ortiz, A. A. (2006). Preventing disproportionate representation: Culturally and linguistically responsive prereferral interventions. *Teaching Exceptional Children, 38*(4), 64–68.

Gauvain, M. (2001). *The social context of cognitive development.* New York: Guilford Press.

Gauvain, M. (2013). Sociocultural contexts of development. In P. D. Zelazo (Ed.), *Oxford handbook of developmental psychology: Vol. 2., Self and other* (pp. 425–451). New York: Oxford University Press.

Gilliam, W. S. (2005). *Prekindergarteners left behind: Expulsion rates in state prekindergarten systems.* New York: Foundation for Child Development. Retrieved from http://challengingbehavior.fmhi.usf.edu/explore/policy_docs/prek_expulsion.pdf

Ginsberg, K. (with Jablow, M. M.). (2015). *Building resilience in children and teens* (2nd ed.). Elk Grove Village, IL: American Academy of Pediatrics.

Gladwell, M. (2013). *David and Goliath: Underdogs, misfits, and the art of battling giants.* Boston: Little, Brown.

Glasser, H. (with Block, M. L.). (2011). *Notching up: The Nurtured Heart approach: The new inner wealth initiative for educators.* Tucson, AZ: Nurtured Heart.

Gonzáles, N., Moll, L. C., & Amanti, C. (Eds.). (2005). *Funds of knowledge: Theorizing practices in households, communities, and classrooms.* Mahwah, NJ: Lawrence Erlbaum.

Gonzáles, N., Moll, L., Tenery, M. F., Rivera, A., Rendon, P., Gonzales, R., & Amanti, C. (2005). Funds of knowledge for teaching in Latino households. In N. Gonzalez, L. Moll, & C. Amanti (Eds.), *Funds of knowledge: Theorizing practices in households, communities, and classrooms* (pp. 89–118). Mahwah, NJ: Lawrence Erlbaum.

Gorski, P. (2008). The myth of the culture of poverty. *Educational Leadership, 65*(7), 32–36. Retrieved from http://www.ascd.org/publications/educational-leadership/apr08/vol65/num07/The-Myth-of-the-Culture-of-Poverty.aspx

Grantmakers for Education. (2013). *Educating English language learners: Grantmaking strategies for closing America's other achievement gap.* Retrieved from https://edfunders.org/sites/default/files/Educating%20English%20Language%20Learners_April%202013.pdf

Grove, T., & Glasser, H. (with Block, M. L.). (2007). *The inner wealth initiative: The Nurtured Heart approach for educators.* Tucson, AZ: Nurtured Heart.

Guo, W., & Tsui, M. (2010). From resilience to resistance: A construction of the strengths perspective in social work practice. *International Social Work, 53,* 233–245.

Gurwitch, R. H., Pfefferbaum, B., Montgomery, J. M., Klomp, R. W., & Reissman, D. B. (2007). *Building community resilience for children and families.* Oklahoma City, OK: Terrorism Disaster Center. Retrieved from http://www.nctsnet.org/nctsn_assets/pdfs/edu_materials/BuildingCommunity_FINAL_02-12-07.pdf

Hammond, Z. (2015). *Culturally responsive teaching and the brain: Promoting authentic engagement and rigor among culturally and linguistically diverse students.* Thousand Oaks, CA: Corwin.

Hattie, J. A. (2008). *Visible learning: A synthesis of over 800 meta-analyses relating to achievement.* New York: Routledge.

Henderson, A., Mapp, K., Johnson, V. R., & Davies, D. (2007). *Beyond the bake sale: The essential guide to family/school partnerships.* New York: New Press.

Hertel, R., & Johnson, M. M. (2013). How the traumatic experiences of students manifest in school settings. In E. Rossen & R. Hull (Eds.), *Supporting and educating traumatized students: A guide for school-based professionals* (pp. 23–35). New York: Oxford University Press.

Johnson, D. W., & Johnson, F. (2009). *Joining together: Group theory and group skills* (10th ed.). Boston: Allyn and Bacon.

Johnson, D. W., Johnson, R., & Holubec, E. (2008). *Cooperation in the classroom* (7th ed.). Edina, MN: Interaction Book.

Kilmer, R. P., Gil-Rivas, V., & Hardy, S. J. (2013). Students responding to natural disasters and terrorism. In E. Rossen & R. Hull (Eds.), *Supporting and educating traumatized students: A guide for school-based professionals* (p. 229–250). New York: Oxford University Press.

Knost, E., & Perry, E. (2016). College and career readiness in the classroom. In K. S. McKnight (Ed.), *Addressing the needs of all learners in the era of changing standards: Helping our most vulnerable students succeed through teaching flexibility, innovation, and creativity* (pp. 199–214). Lanham, MD: Rowman & Littlefield.

Kral, R. (1989). *Strategies that work: Techniques for solution in the schools.* Milwaukee, WI: Brief Family Therapy Center, Wisconsin Institute on Family Studies.

Lawrence-Lightfoot, S. (2003). *The essential conversation: What parents and teachers can learn from each other.* New York: Random House.

Lerner, R. M., Almerigi, J. B., Theokas, C., & Lerner, J. V. (2005). Positive youth development: A view of the issues. *Journal of Early Adolescence, 25*(1), 10–16.

Lotan, R. A. (2006). Teaching teachers to build equitable classrooms. *Theory into Practice, 45*(1), 32–39.

Mahar, M. T., Murphy, S. K., Rowe, D. A., Golden, J., Shields, A. T., & Raedeke, T. D. (2006). Effects of a classroom-based program on physical activity and on-task behavior. *Medicine & Science in Sports & Exercise, 38,* 2086–2094.

Marshall, H. W., & DeCapua, A. (2014). *Making the transition to the classroom: Culturally responsive teaching for struggling language learners.* Ann Arbor, MI: University of Michigan Press.

Maslow, A. H. (1999). *Toward a psychology of being* (3rd ed.). New York: John Wiley & Sons.

Masten, A. S., & Coatsworth, J. D. (1998). The development of competence in favorable and unfavorable environments: Lessons from research on successful children. *American Psychologist, 53*(2), 205–220.

Menjívar, C., & Cervantes, A. G. (2016, November). The effects of parental undocumented status on families and children. Retrieved from http://www.apa.org/pi/families/resources/newsletter/2016/11/undocumented-status.aspx

Mind Matters. (n.d.). Empowering students. Retrieved from https://www.mindmatters.edu.au/explore-modules/empowering-students

Moll, L., Amanti, C., Neff, D., & Gonzalez, N. (1992). Funds of knowledge for teaching: Using a qualitative approach to connect homes and classrooms. *Theory Into Practice, 31*(1), 131–141.

Morris, C. G., & Maisto, A. A. (2002). *Psychology: An introduction* (11th ed.). New York: Pearson Education.

National Child Traumatic Stress Network. (2008). *Pathways to partnerships with youth and families in the National Child Traumatic Stress Network.* Retrieved from http://www.nctsn.org/nctsn_assets/pdfs/Pathways_ver_finished.pdf

National Institutes of Health. (2016). The epidemiology of traumatic event exposure worldwide: Results from the World Mental Health Survey Consortium. Retrieved from: https://www.ncbi.nlm.nih.gov/pmc/articles/PMC4869975/

Otto, M. (2007, February 27). For want of a dentist. *Washington Post.* Retrieved from http://www.washingtonpost.com/wp-dyn/content/article/2007/02/27/AR2007022702116.html

Paden-Dowdell, L. (2016). *New Americans class: Community circle time.* Retrieved from https://www.youtube.com/watch?v=Om84NSNUYB0&feature=youtu.be

Pearson, P. D., & Gallagher, M. (1983). The instruction of reading comprehension. *Contemporary Educational Psychology, 8,* 317–344.

Perry, B., & Szalavitz, M. (2006). *The boy who was raised as a dog: What traumatized children can teach us about loss, love, and healing.* New York: Basic Books.

Pink, D. H. (2009). *Drive: The surprising truth about what motivates us.* New York: Penguin Press.

Presidential Task Force on Posttraumatic Stress Disorder and Trauma in Children and Adolescents. (2008). Children and trauma. Retrieved from http://www.apa.org/pi/families/resources/children-trauma-update.aspx

Pulla, V. (2012). What are strengths based practices all about? In V. Pulla, L. Chenoweth, A. Francis, & S. Bakaj (Eds.), *Papers in strength based practice* (pp. 1–18). New Delhi, India: Allied.

Quaglia, R. J., & Corso, M. J. (2014). *Student voice: The instrument of change.* Thousand Oaks, CA: Corwin.

Rapp, C. A. (1998). *The strengths model: Case management with people suffering from severe and persistent mental illness.* Oxford, UK: Oxford University Press.

Rogoff, B. (1990). *Apprenticeship in thinking: Cognitive development in social context.* New York: Oxford University Press.

Rogoff, B. (2003). *The cultural nature of human development.* New York: Oxford University Press.

Roland, D., & Matheson, D. (2012). New theory from an old technique: The Rolma matrices. *The Clinical Teacher, 9,* 143–147.

Rossen, E., & Hull, R. (Eds). (2013). *Supporting and educating traumatized students: A guide for school-based professionals.* New York: Oxford University Press.

Saint-Jacques, M. C., Turcotte, D., & Pouliot, E. (2009). Adopting a strengths perspective in social work practice with families in difficulty: From theory to practice. *Families in Society, 9*(4), 454–461. doi:10.1606/1044-3894.3926

Saleebey, D. (1996). *The strengths perspective in social work practice.* New York: Longman.

Saleebey, D. (2000). Power in the people: Strengths and hope. *Advances in Social Work, 1*(2), 127–136.

Santiago, E., Yanosy, S., Ferrara, J., & Harrison, L. (2016). *The sanctuary classroom companion planner.* Yonkers, NY: Sanctuary Institute.

Seligman, M. E. P., Rashid, T., & Parks, A. C. (2006). Positive psychotherapy. *American Psychologist, 61*(8), 774–788. http://dx.doi.org/10.1037/0003-066X.61.8.774

Sharan, S. (1990). *Cooperative learning theory and research.* New York: Praeger.

Silverstone, M., & Zacarian, D. (2012). Grade two: Evens and odds, how many in all? In M. Gottlieb & G. Slavit Ernst (Eds.), *Academic language in diverse classrooms: Mathematics: Grade K-2: Promoting content and language learning* (pp. 129–162). Thousand Oaks, CA: Corwin Press.

Steele, C. M. (2010). *Whistling Vivaldi and other clues to how stereotypes affect us.* New York: W. W. Norton.

Toshalis, E., & Nakkula, M. J. (2012). *Motivation, engagement, and student voice.* Boston: Jobs for the Future.

Tosolt, B. (2008). *Middle school students' perceptions of caring teacher behaviors: An empirical analysis by student minority status* (Doctoral dissertation). Retrieved from ProQuest Dissertations. (3333077)

Tosolt, B. (2009). Middle school students' perceptions of caring teacher behaviors: Differences by minority status. *Journal of Negro Education, 78,* 405–416.

Tyler, K. M., Uqdah, A. L., Dillihunt, M. L., Beatty-Hazelbaker, R., Conner, T., Gadson, N. C., . . . Stevens, R. (2008). Cultural discontinuity: Toward a quantitative investigation of a major hypothesis in education. *Educational Researcher, 37*(5), 280–297.

U.S. Customs and Border Patrol. (2015). Southwest border unaccompanied alien children FY 2014. Retrieved from https://www.cbp.gov/newsroom/stats/southwest-border-unaccompanied-children/fy-2014

U.S. Department of Education. (2015). Family Educational Rights and Privacy Act (FERPA). Retrieved from http://www2.ed.gov/policy/gen/guid/fpco/ferpa/index.html

U.S. Department of State. (2015). Cumulative summary of refugee admissions. Retrieved from https://2009-2017.state.gov/j/prm/releases/statistics/251288.htm

Valencia, R. R. (2010). *Dismantling contemporary deficit thinking: Educational thought and practice.* New York: Routledge.

Vygotsky, L. (1978). *Mind in society* (M. Cole, Trans.). Cambridge, MA: Harvard University Press.

WETA Public Broadcasting. (2017a). Connie Phelps Bozek. Retrieved from http://www.colorincolorado.org/videos/classroom-videos/community-schools-and-ells/connie-phelps-bozek

WETA Public Broadcasting. (2017b). Dr. Clemencia Vargas. Retrieved from http://www.colorincolorado.org/dr-clemencia-vargas

WETA Public Broadcasting. (2017c). How a community school helps ELLs succeed. Retrieved from http://www.colorincolorado.org/videos/classroom-videos/community-schools-and-ells

Wiebler, L. R. (2013). Developmental differences in response to trauma. In E. Rossen & R. Hull (Eds.), *Supporting and educating traumatized students: A guide for school-based professionals* (pp. 39–47). New York: Oxford University Press.

Willett, J., Bailey, F., Jeannot, M., & Zacarian, D. (1998). *The discursive construction of authority in cooperative learning.* Paper presented at the 10th Annual Conference on Ethnographic and Qualitative Research in Education, Amherst, MA.

Yonezawa, S., & Jones, M. (2009). Student voices: Generating reform from the inside out. *Theory Into Practice, 48,* 205–212.

Yoshikawa, H. (2011). *Immigrants raising citizens: Undocumented parents and their children.* New York: Russell Sage Foundation.

Young, D. (2002). Classroom environment: The basics. Learn NC: K-12 Teaching and Learning from the UNC School of Education. Retrieved from http://www.learnnc.org/lp/pages/734?ref=search

Zacarian, D. (2011). *Transforming schools for English learners: A comprehensive framework for school leaders.* Thousand Oaks, CA: Corwin.

Zacarian, D. (2013). *Mastering academic language: A framework for supporting student achievement.* Thousand Oaks, CA: Corwin.

Zacarian, D., & Haynes, J. (2012). *The essential guide for educating beginning English learners.* Thousand Oaks, CA: Corwin.

Zacarian, D., & Lukens, L. (2016, April). *Reaching English learners living with trauma and chronic stress.* Panel discussion presented at the annual meeting of TESOL International Association, Baltimore, MD.

Zacarian, D., & Silverstone, M. (2015). *In it together: How student, family, and community partnerships advance engagement and achievement in diverse classrooms.* Thousand Oaks, CA: Corwin.

Index

The letter *f* following a page number denotes a figure.

About the Authors

Debbie Zacarian, EdD, is known for her work in advancing student achievement. Her explanations of current research into practical instructional, leadership, family-school engagement, and strength-based teacher evaluation systems are nationally known and widely practiced. With an advanced degree in clinical psychology and a doctorate in educational policy, research, and administration and over three decades of combined experience as a district administrator, university faculty member, and educational service agency leader, she founded Zacarian & Associates. She presents and publishes extensively on working successfully with culturally and linguistically diverse populations, including working with students living with trauma, violence, and chronic stress. Her authored and coauthored books include *In It Together: How Student, Family, and Community Partnerships Advance Engagement and Achievement in Diverse Classrooms*; *Mastering Academic Language: A Framework for Supporting Student Achievement*; *Transforming Schools for English Learners: A Comprehensive Framework for School Leaders*; *The Essential Guide for Educating Beginning English Learners*; and *Teaching English Language Learners Across the Content Areas*. Zacarian can be reached at Debbie@zacarian consulting.com.

Lourdes Alvarez-Ortiz, PhD, is a highly accomplished bilingual/bicultural school psychologist with more than two decades of experience working in inner-city school districts serving culturally and linguistically diverse student and family populations. In addition to her expertise assessing and supporting students' socio-emotional and academic growth, she has collaboratively led initiatives supporting teachers and administrators in their efforts to optimize students' potential, work successfully with families, and use culturally responsive practices. Alvarez-Ortiz has also made significant contributions to the educational nonprofit sector, where she has been an outstanding school leader in creating a safe, supportive, engaging, and asset-based school culture. Working in partnership with public school districts, she successfully pioneered innovative educational reform initiatives targeted at improving opportunities and outcomes for students and schools/districts deemed at risk of failure. At the center of Alvarez-Ortiz's work is the relentless pursuit of students', families', educators', and communities' strengths that empower them to capitalize on their potential. She can be reached at lalvarezortiz@icloud.com.

 **Judie Haynes** is a renowned ESL teacher with 28 years' experience working in urban and suburban settings with diverse students and their families. She brings depth of knowledge and practice teaching students and working with families who have experienced trauma, violence, and chronic stress and has supported many school districts in designing and implementing curriculum for students who have experienced these phenomena. She provides extensive professional development throughout the United States on working with English learners and presents at international TESOL and various TESOL affiliates in the United States and Canada. Haynes is the author and coauthor of seven books—the more recent two with Debbie Zacarian titled *The Essential Guide for Educating Beginning English Learners* and *Teaching English Language Learners Across the Content Areas*. She writes a biweekly blog for TESOL and is the cofounder and comoderator of #ELLCHAT, a widely known Twitter chat for teachers of English learners. She can be reached at judieh@optonline.net.

Acknowledgments

We express our gratitude to the following professionals who generously provided us with rich, detailed examples from the field: Kelley Brown, Larry Ferlazzo, JoAnne Ferrara, Mark Gaither, Chris Homiak, Tina Kern, Kathy Lobo, Laura Lukens, Keith Malletta, Marvin Quiñones, Eileen Santiago, Michael Silverstone, Molly Ticknor, and Sarah Yanosy.

We thank our editors Carol Collins and Liz Wegner for their outstanding support and encouragement and our copy editor Sarah Duffy and senior graphic designer Donald Ely for making our writing shine.

We are also deeply grateful to our spouses, families, and friends who supported us with patience and love.

Related ASCD Resources

At the time of publication, the following resources were available (ASCD stock numbers in parentheses).

Print Products

Fostering Resilient Learners: Strategies for Creating a Trauma-Sensitive Classroom by Kristin Souers with Pete Hall (#116014)

Teaching English Language Learners Across the Content Areas by Judie Haynes and Debbie Zacarian (#109032)

Getting Started with English Language Learners: How Educators Can Meet the Challenge by Judie Haynes (#106048)

The Formative Five: Fostering Grit, Empathy, and Other Success Skills Every Student Needs by Thomas R. Hoerr (#116043)

Encouragement in the Classroom: How do I help students stay positive and focused? (ASCD Arias) by Joan Young (#SF114049)

For up-to-date information about ASCD resources, go to **www.ascd.org**. You can search the complete archives of *Educational Leadership* at **www.ascd.org/el**.

ASCD EDge® Group

Exchange ideas and connect with other educators on the social networking site ASCD EDge at http://ascdedge.ascd.org/

ASCD myTeachSource®

Download resources from a professional learning platform with hundreds of research-based best practices and tools for your classroom at http://myteach source.ascd.org/

For more information, send an e-mail to member@ascd.org; call 1-800-933-2723 or 703-578-9600; send a fax to 703-575-5400; or write to Information Services, ASCD, 1703 N. Beauregard St., Alexandria, VA 22311-1714 USA.